▲ ART THERAPY COLORING

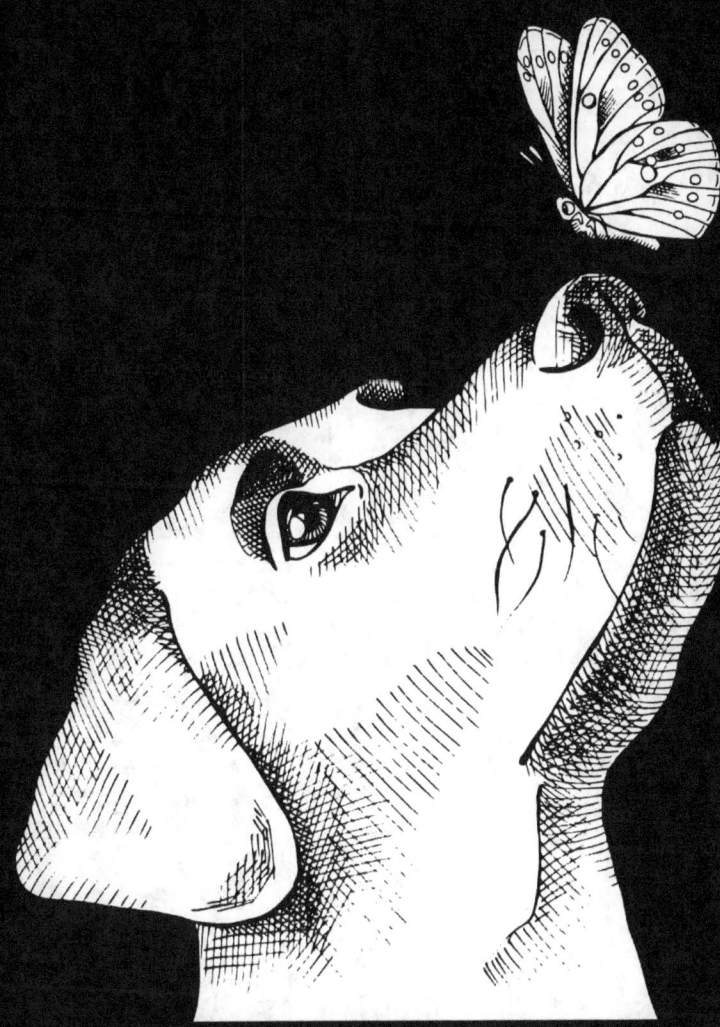

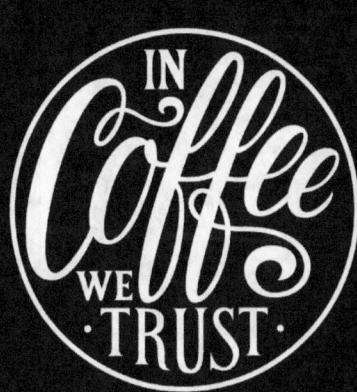

IN Coffee WE ·TRUST·

DOG & COFFEE COLORING BOOK FOR ADULTS

Preview of Coloring Pages

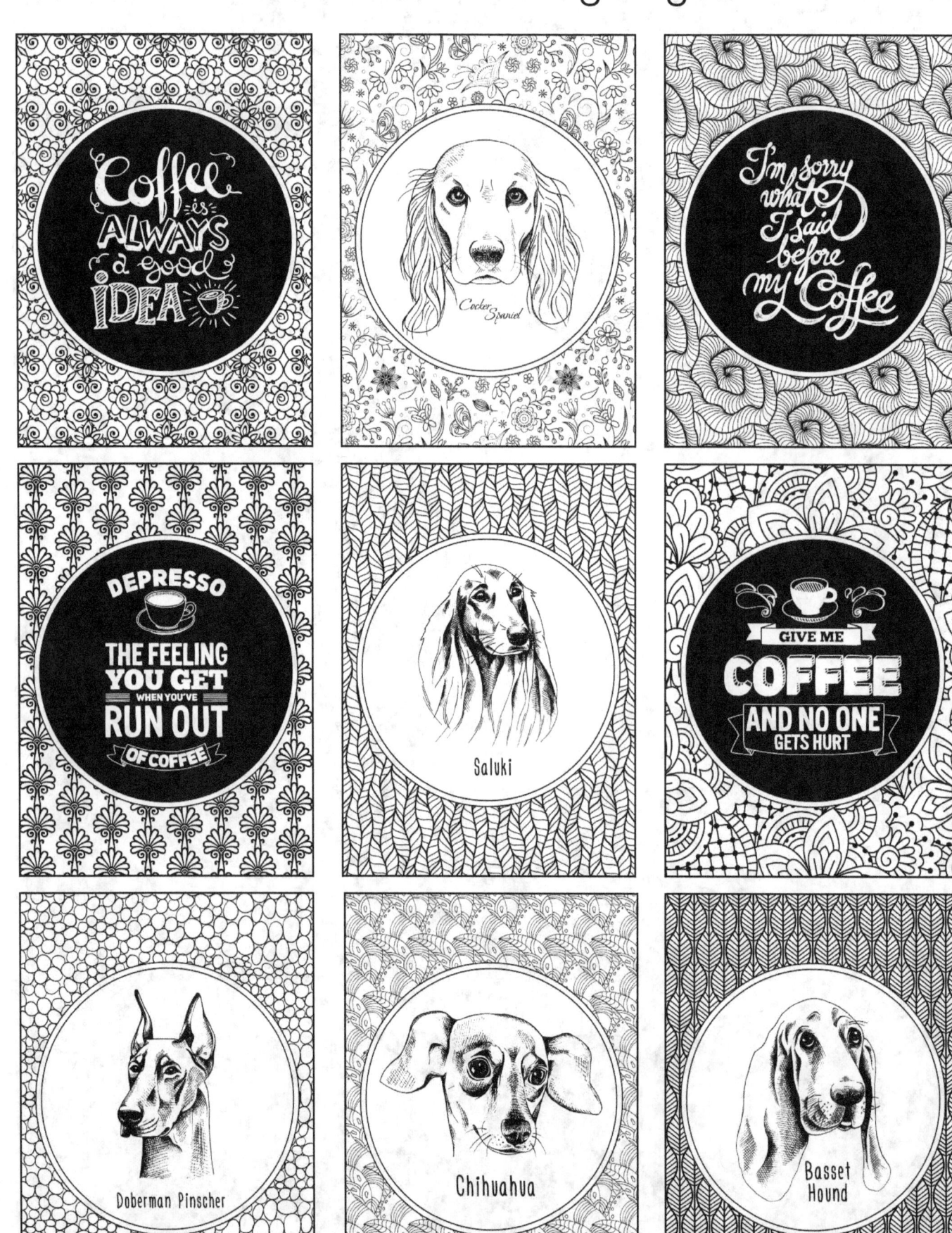

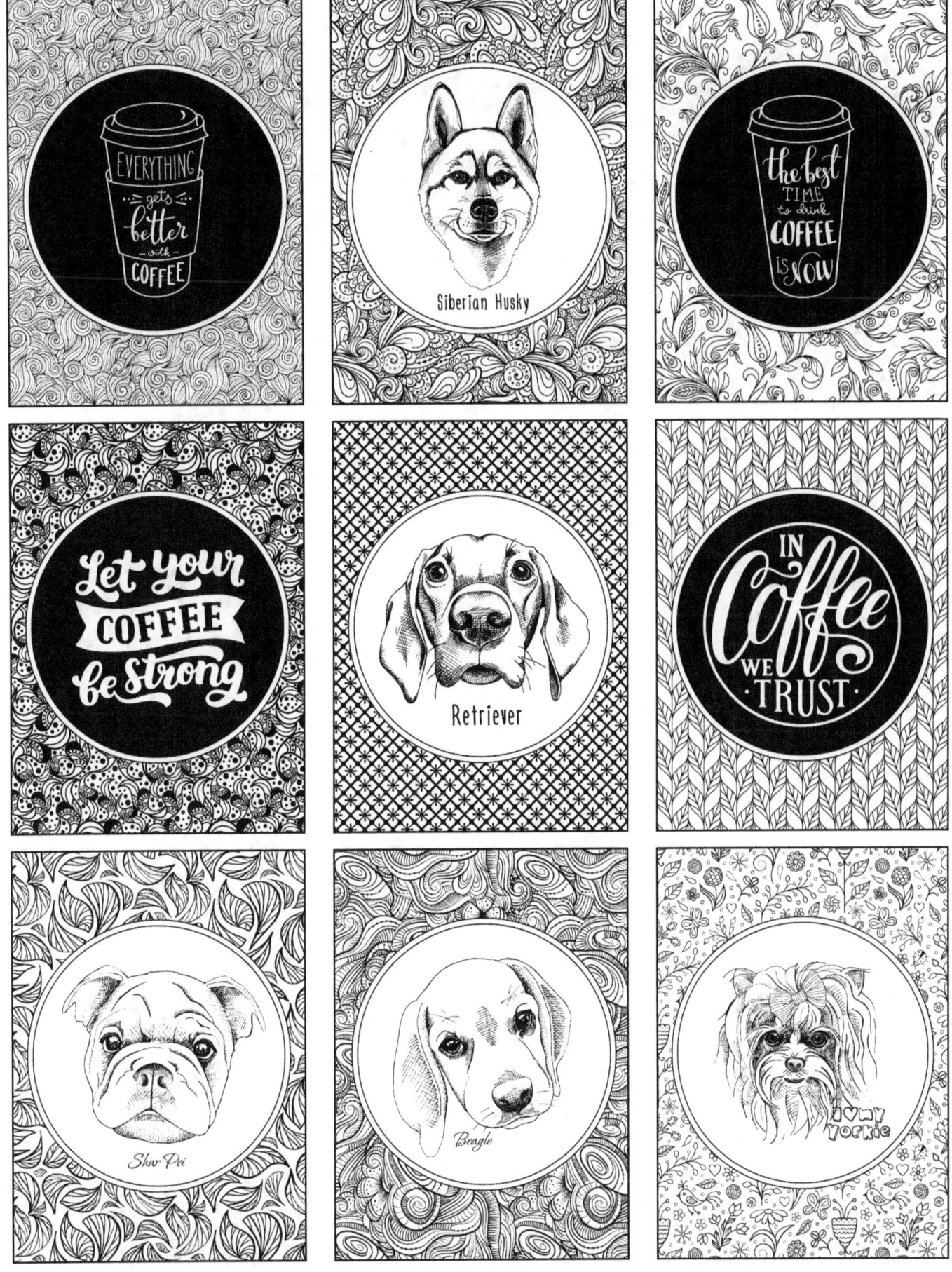

Preview of Coloring Pages

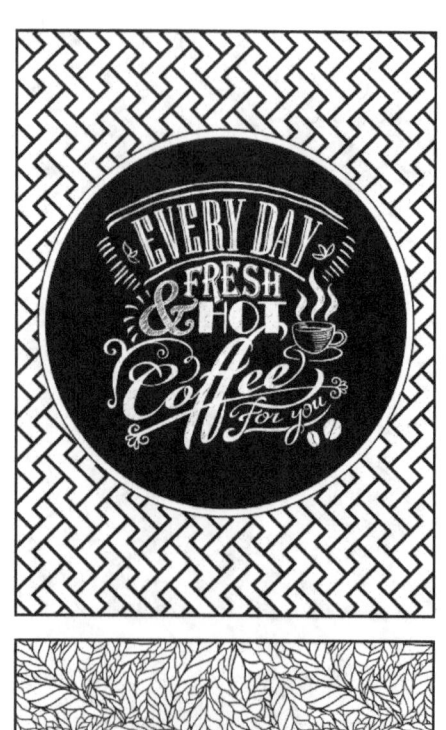

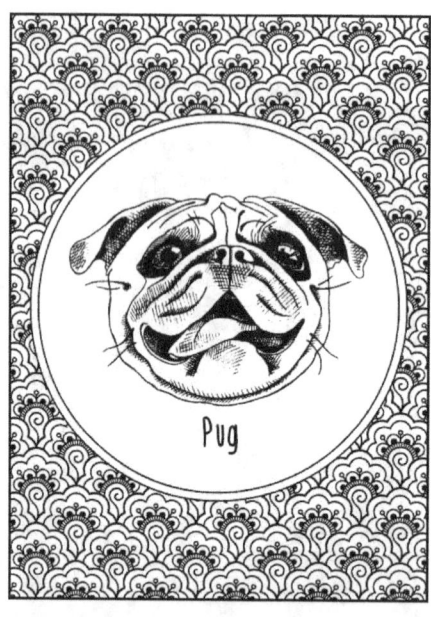

Pug

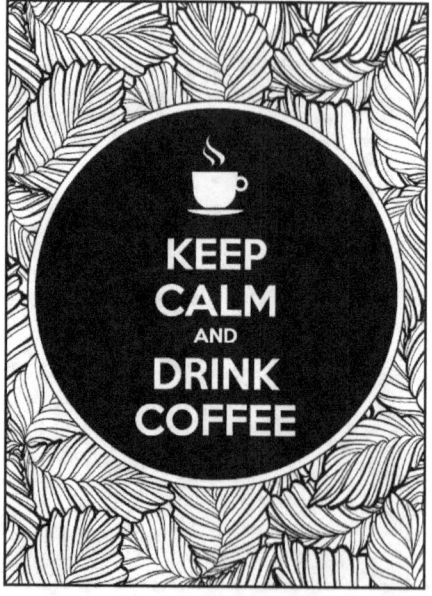

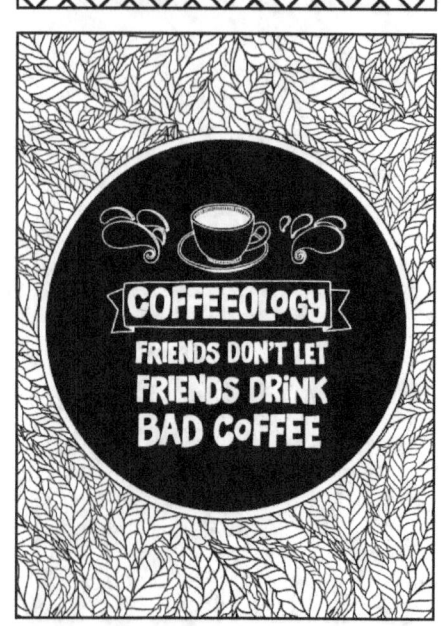

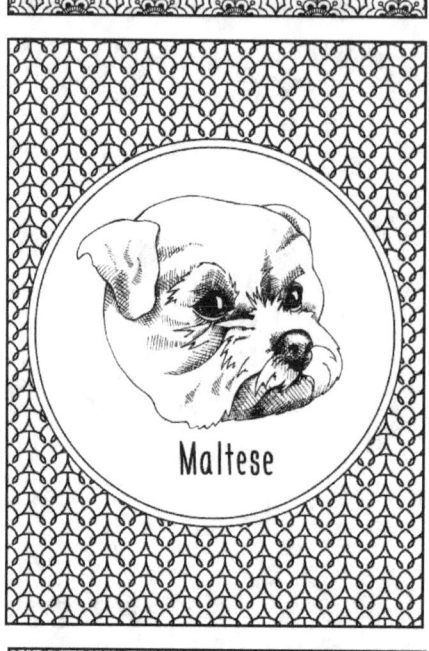

Maltese

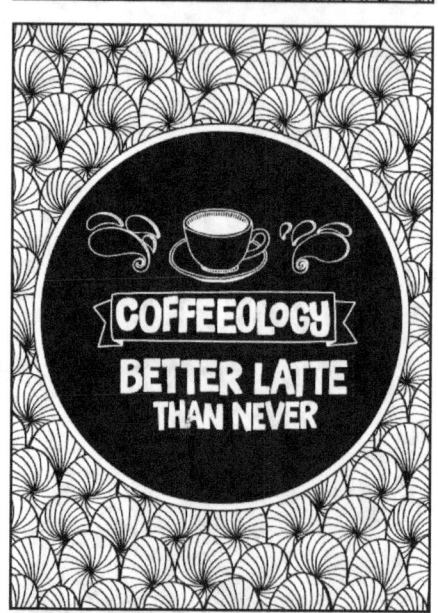

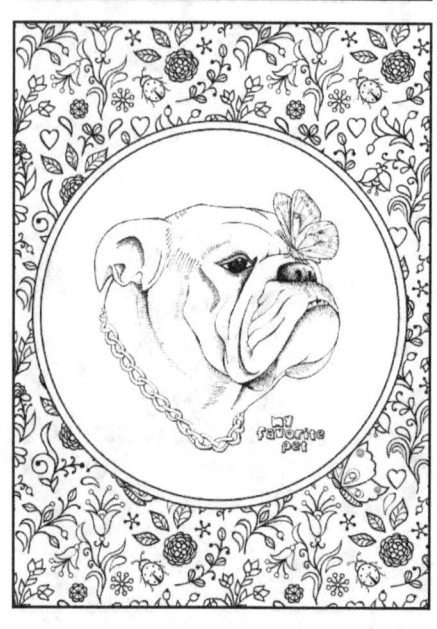

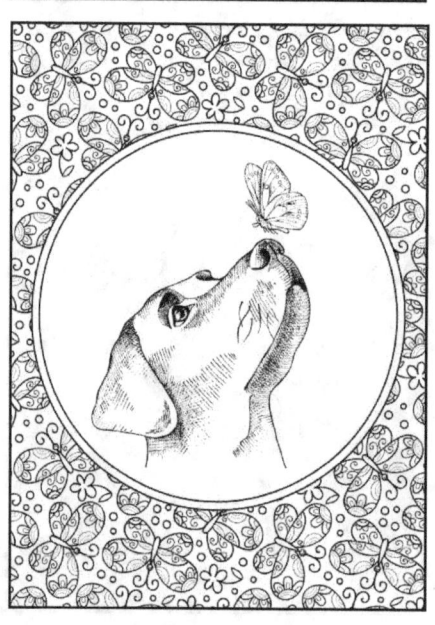

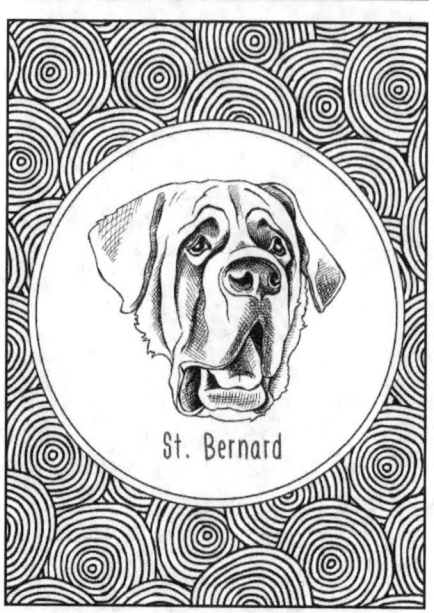

St. Bernard

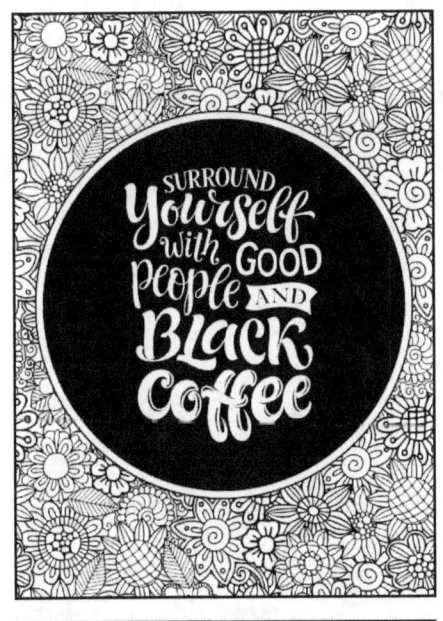

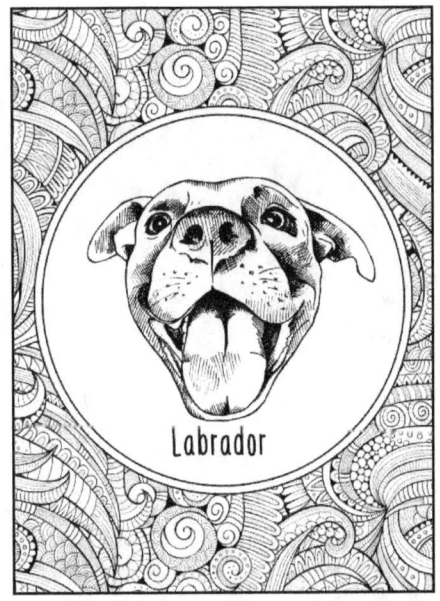

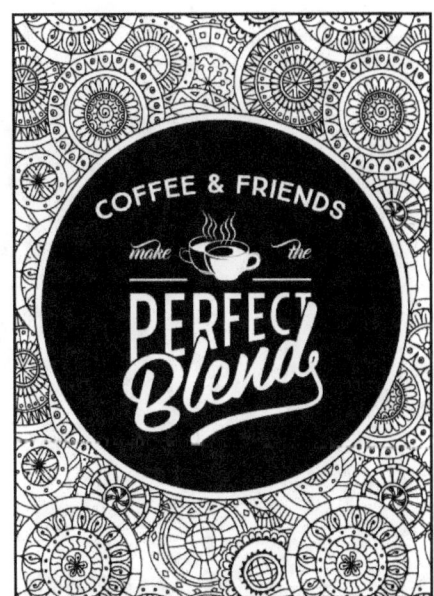

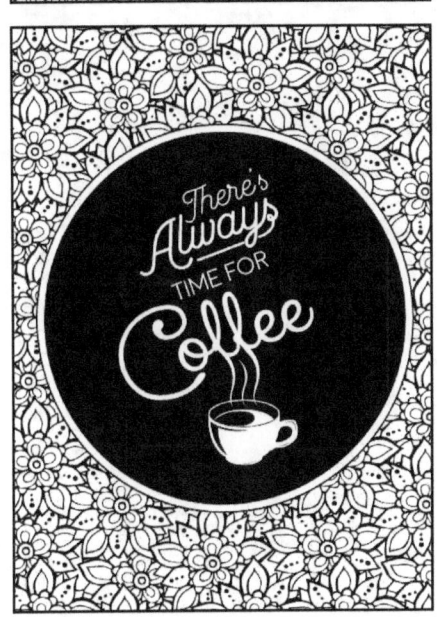

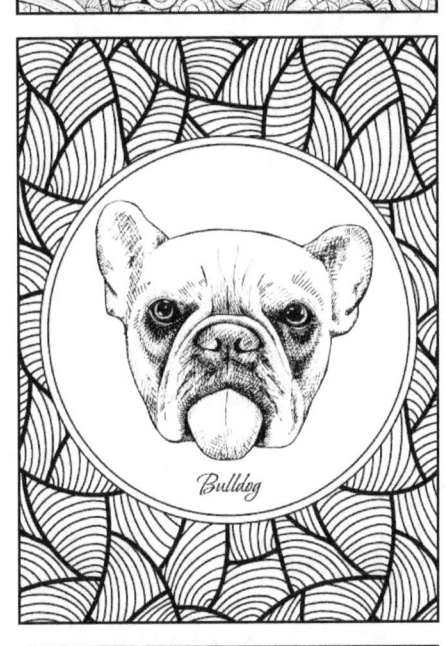

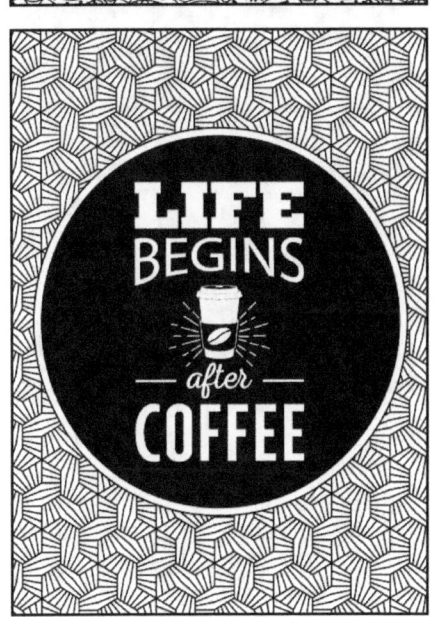

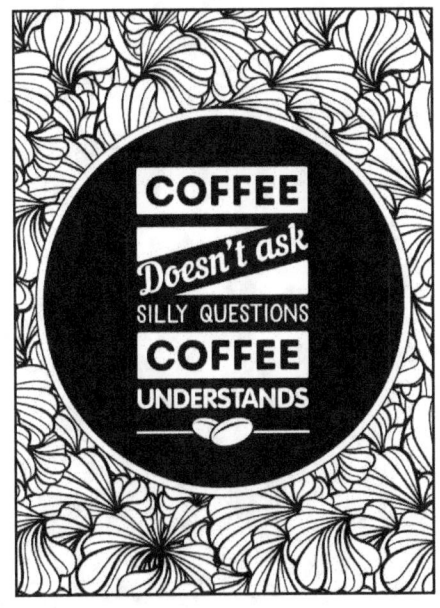

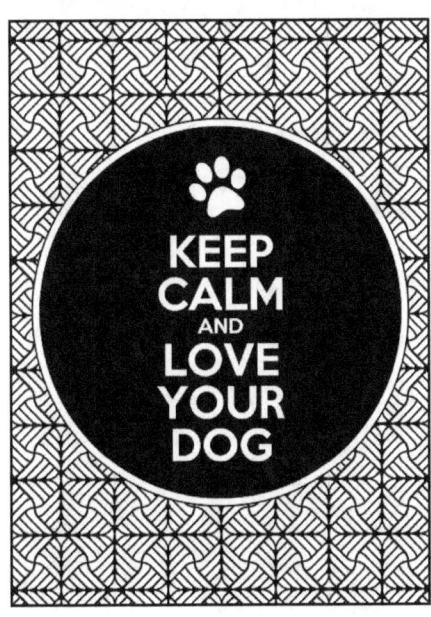

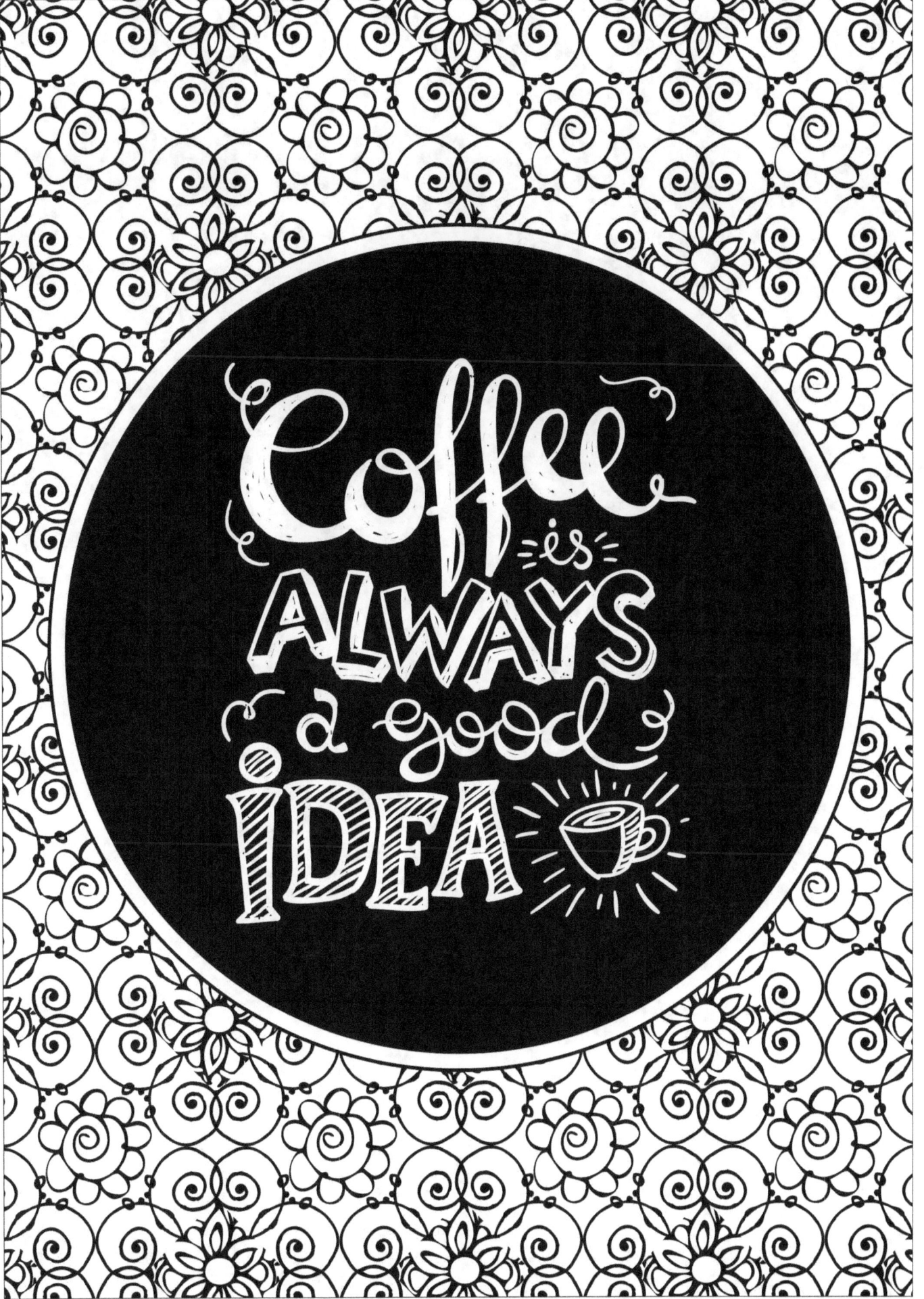

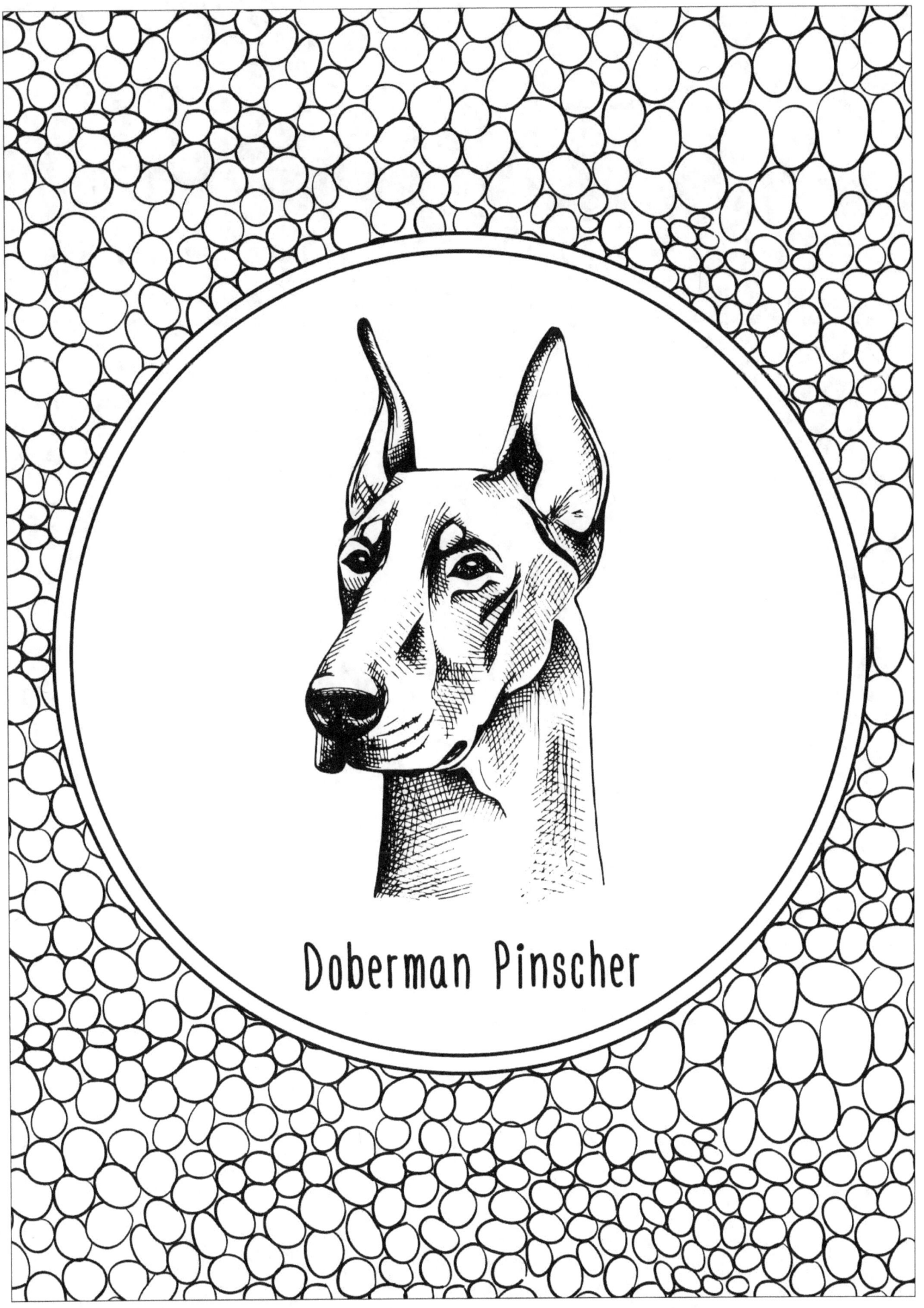

Doberman Pinscher

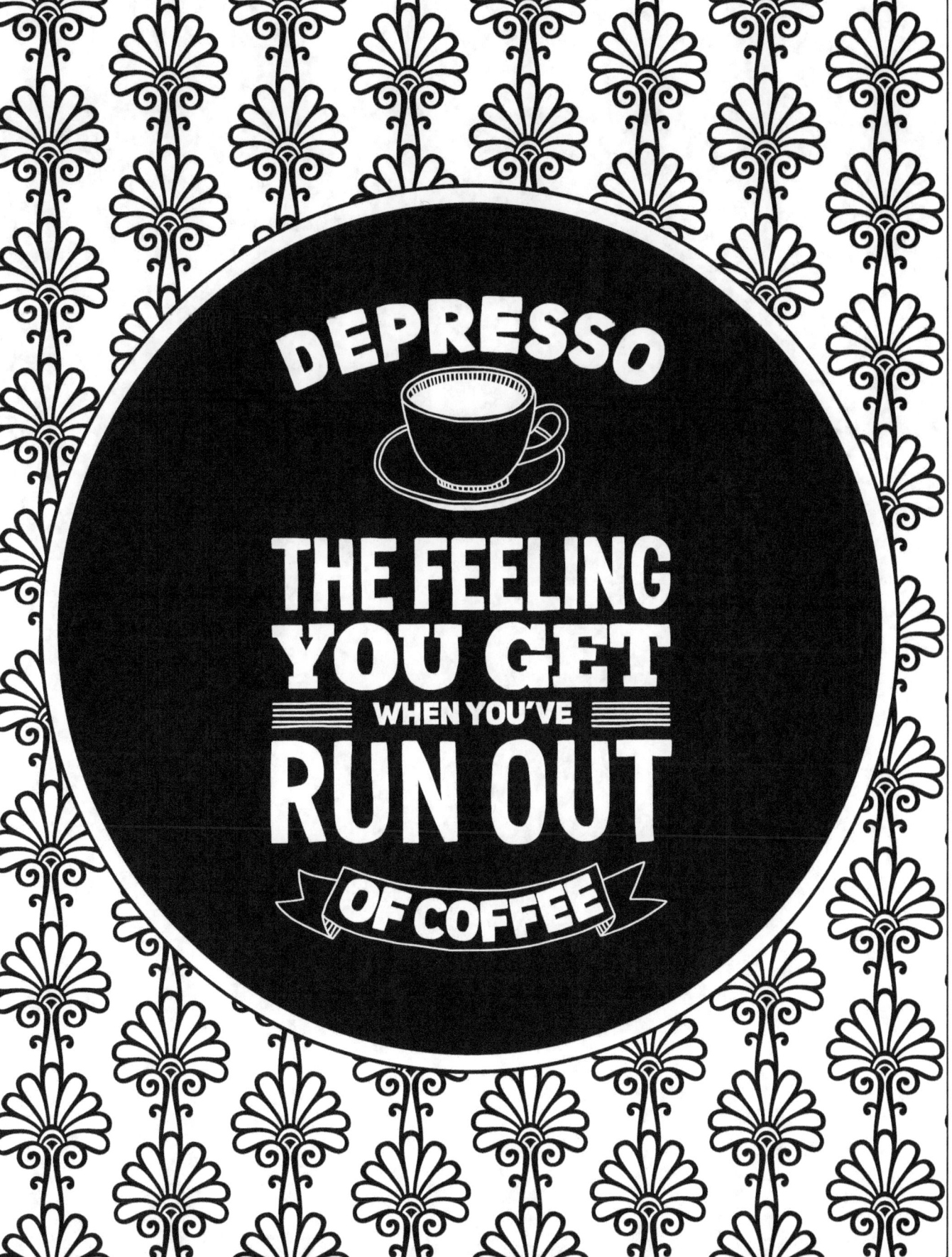

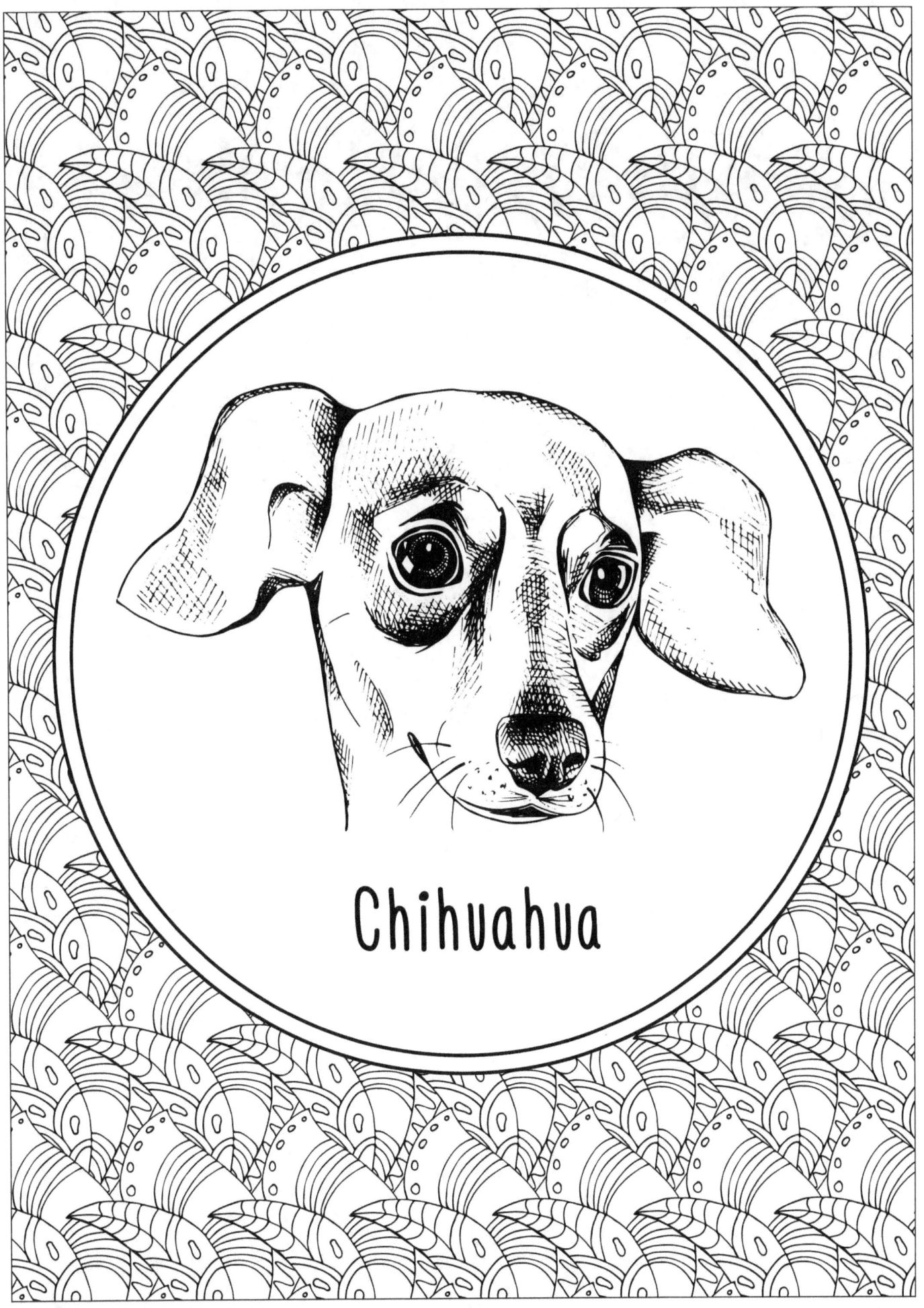

Chihuahua

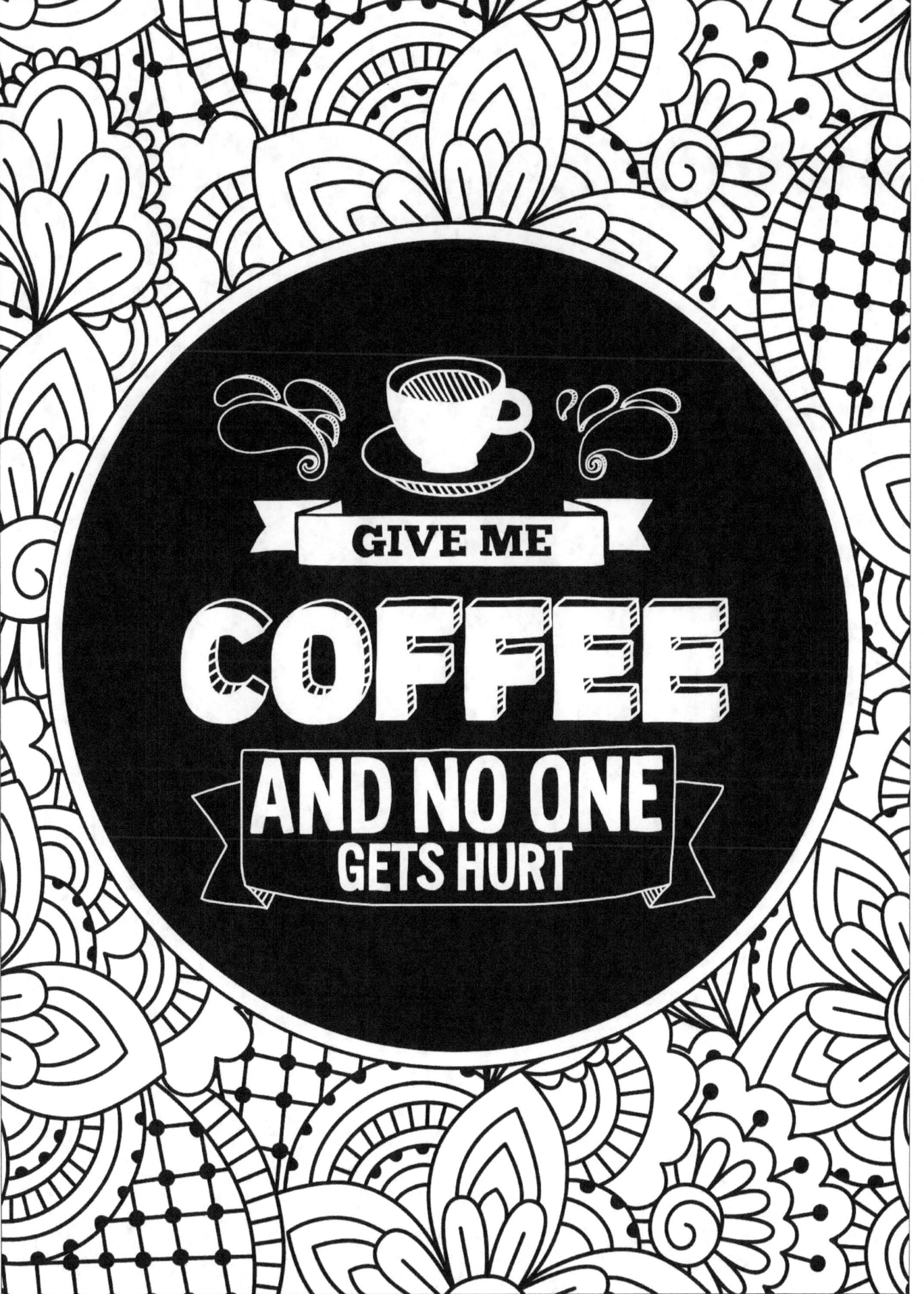

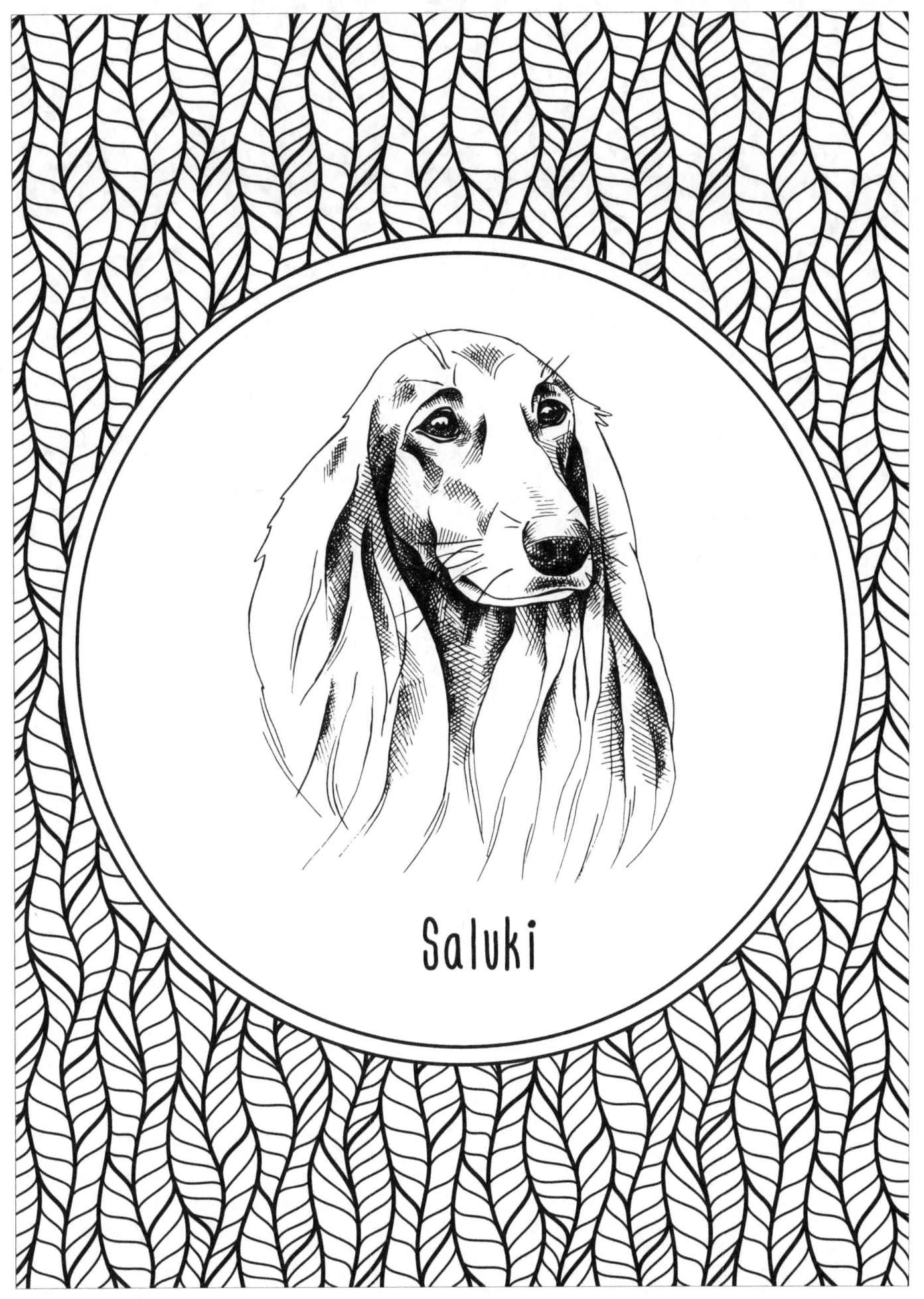

Saluki

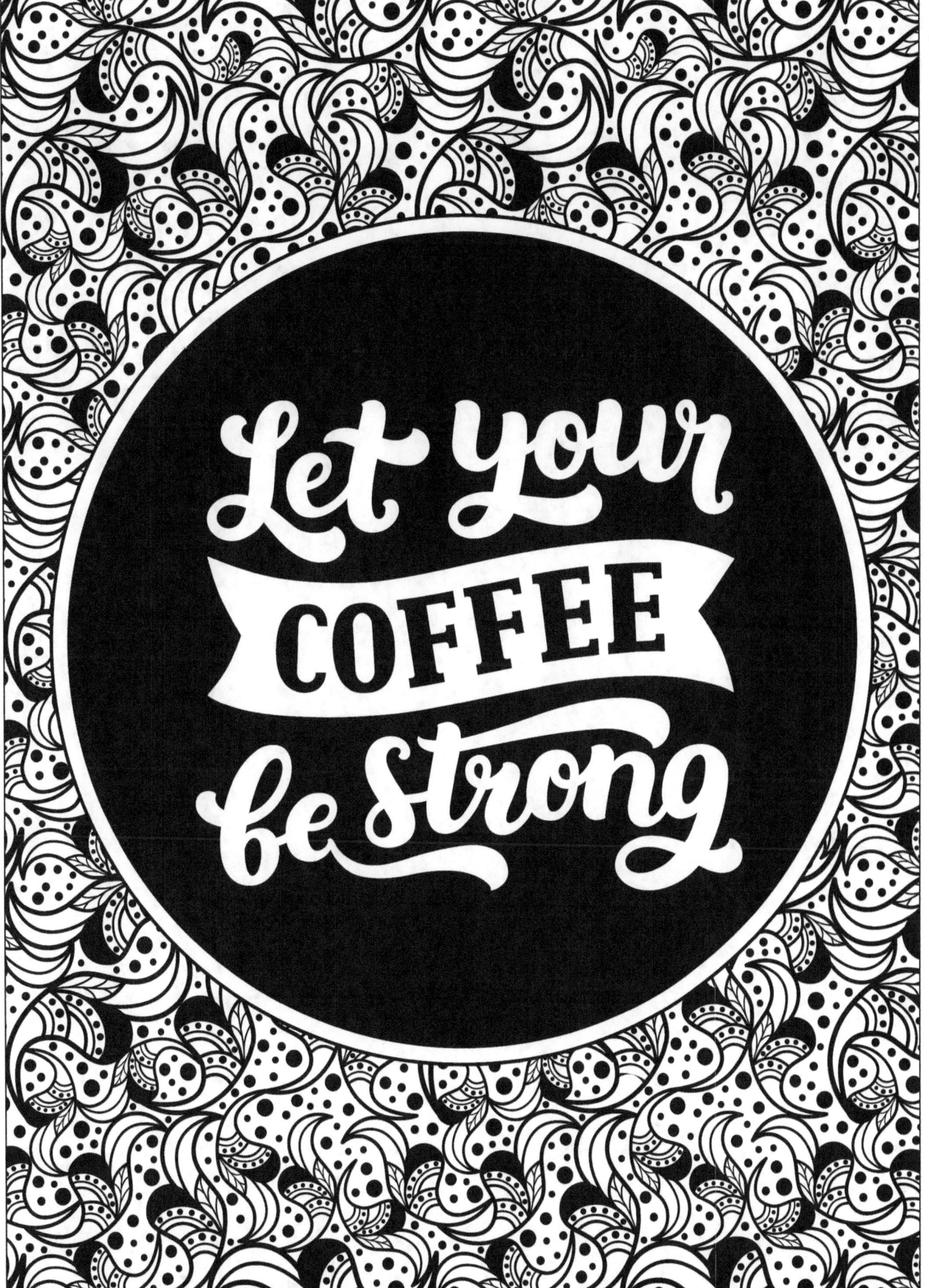

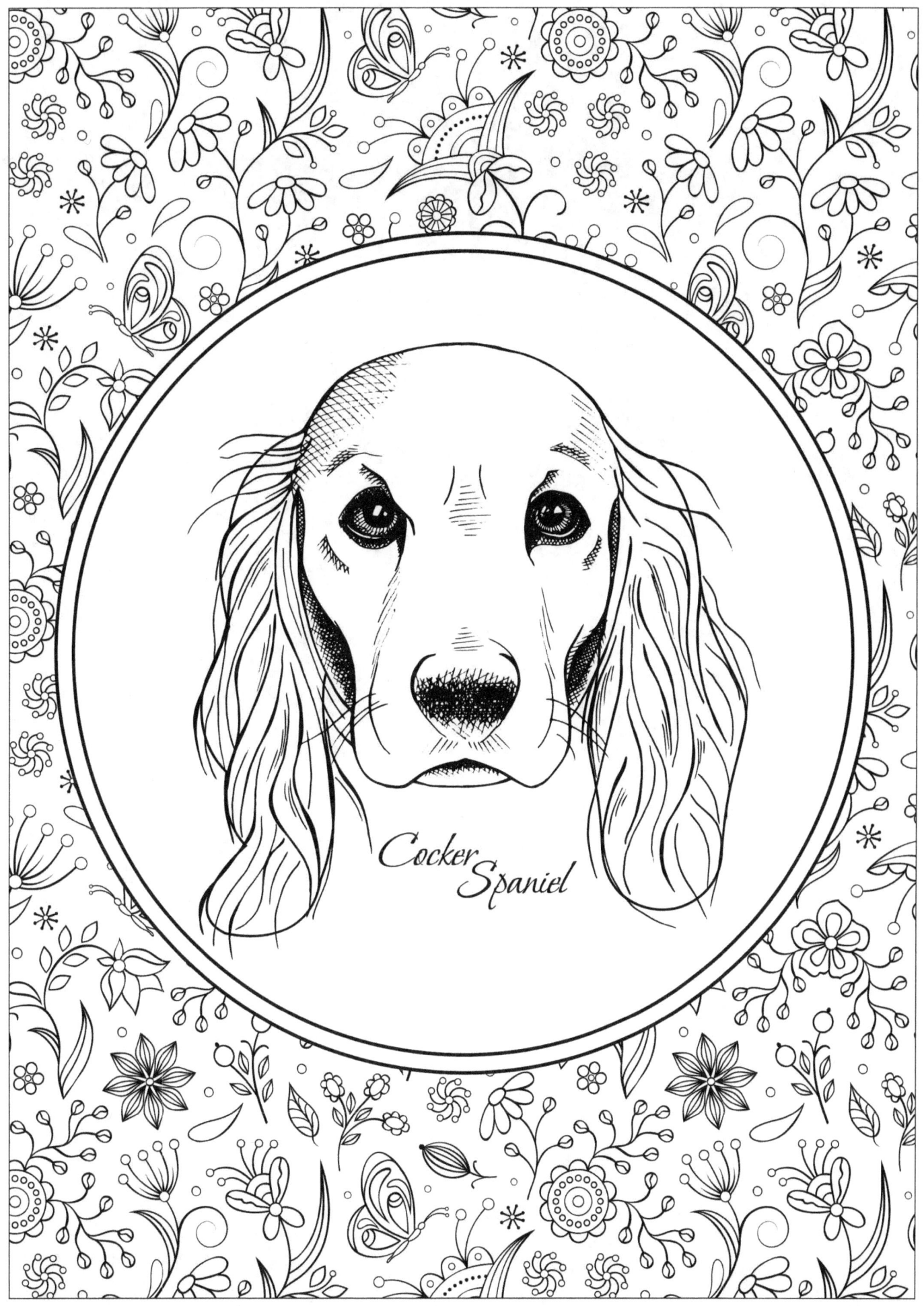

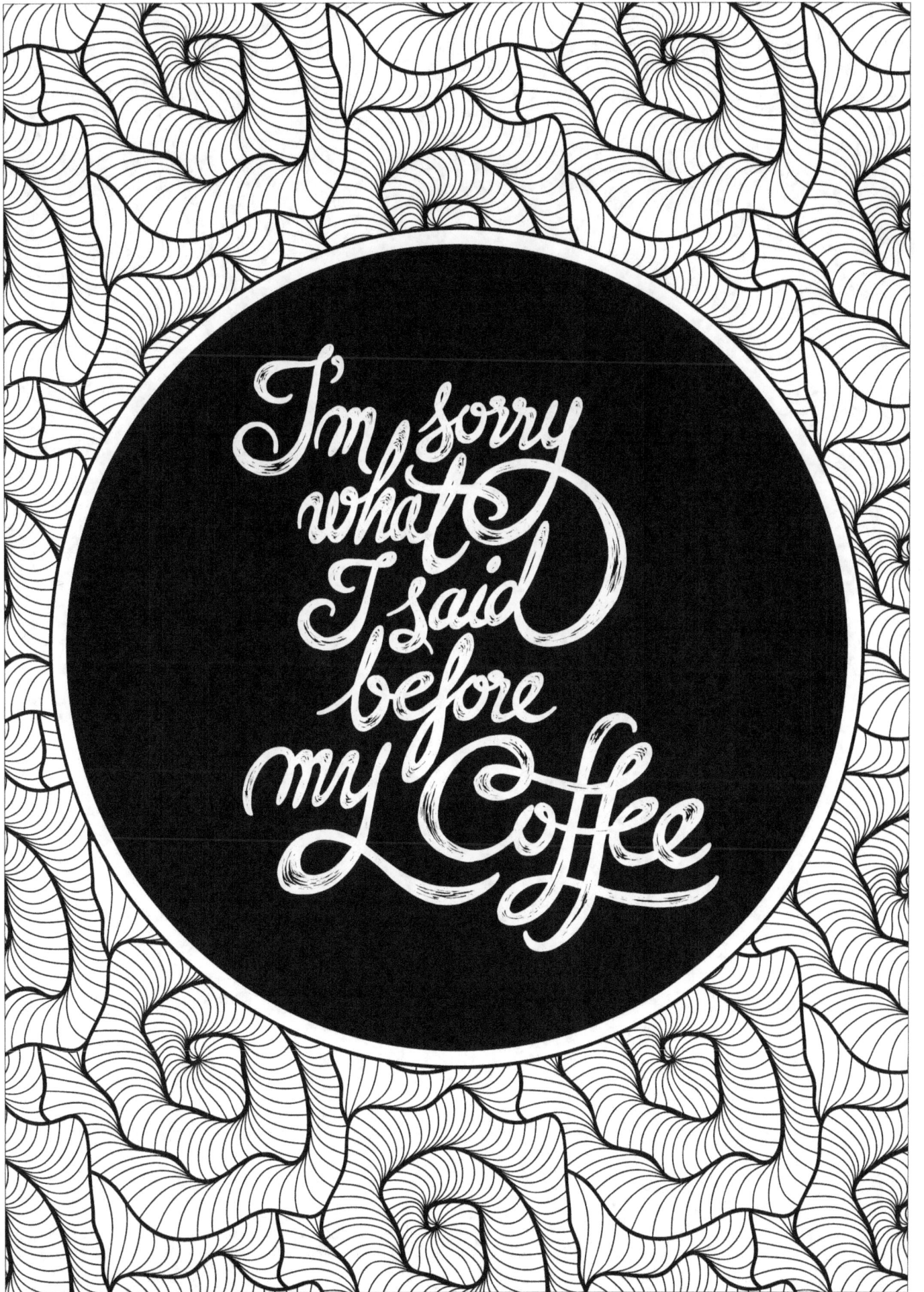

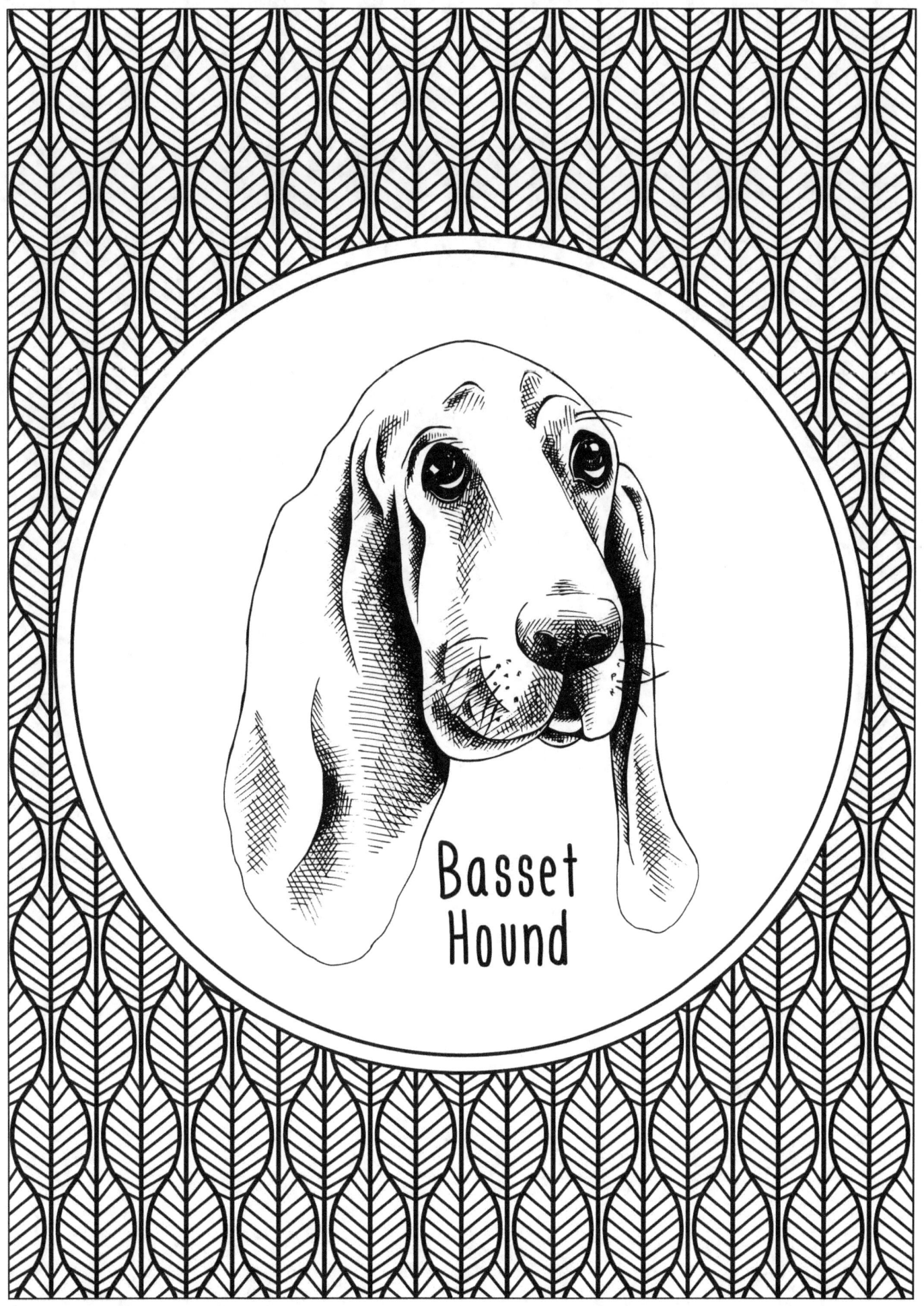

Basset
Hound

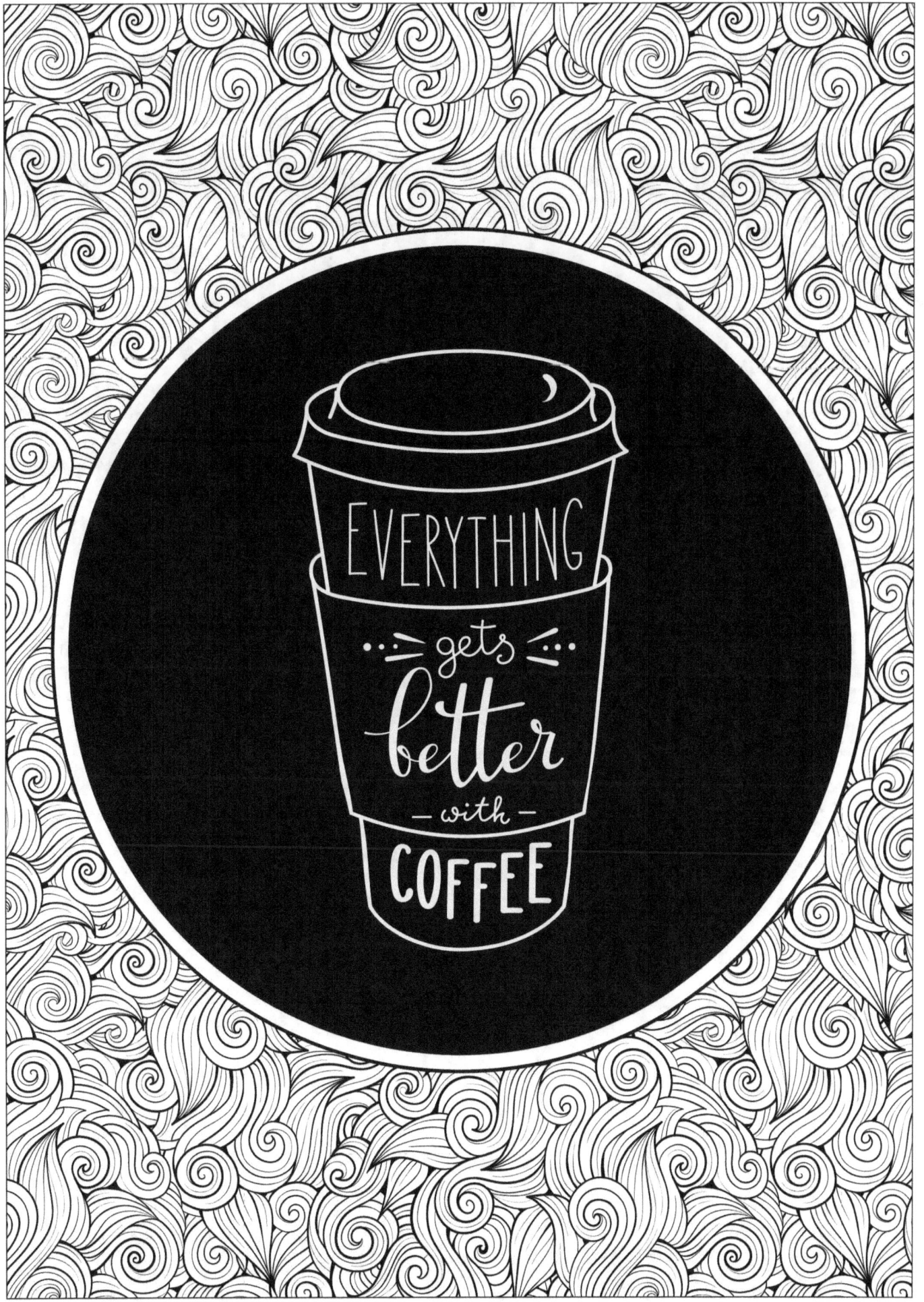

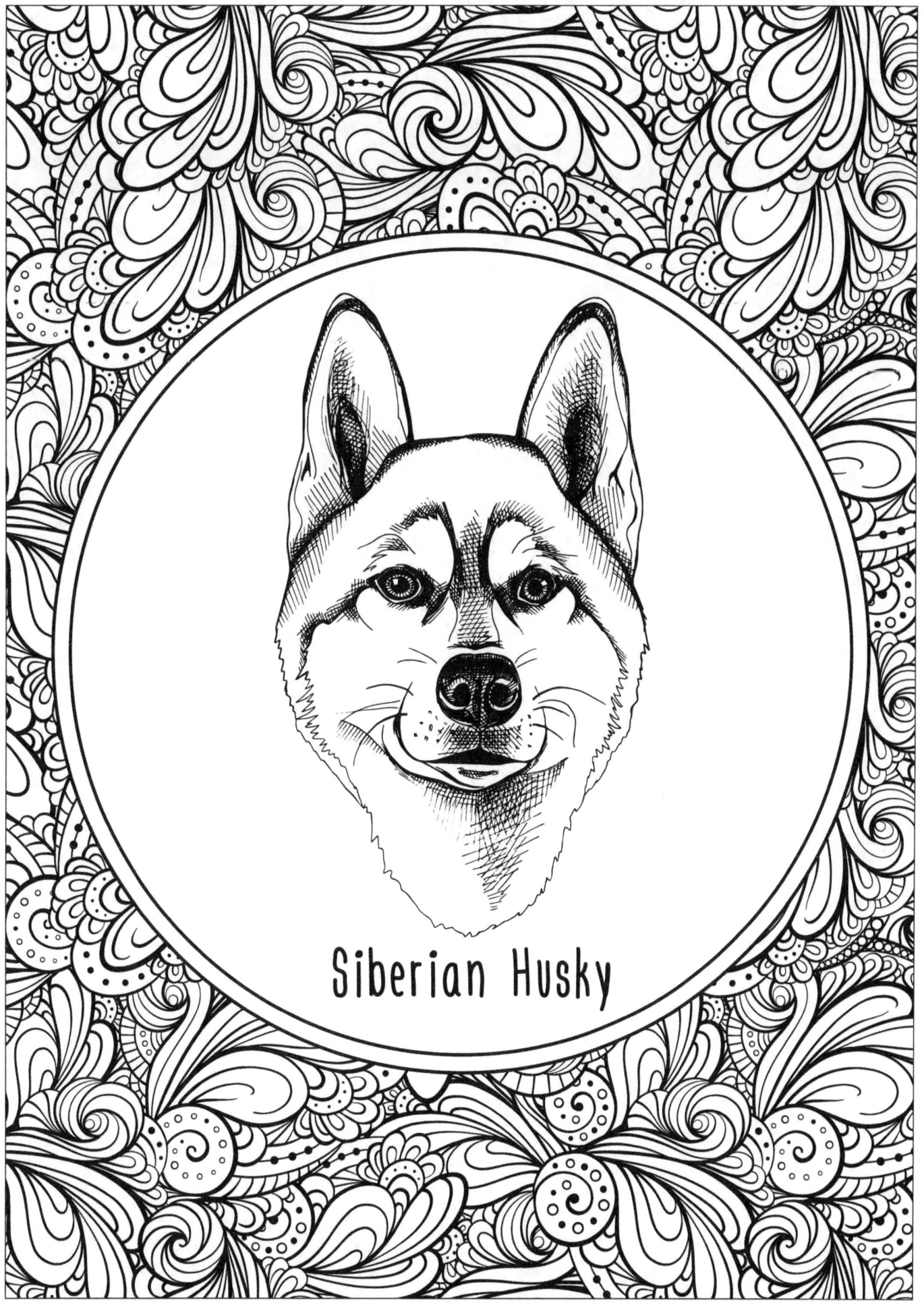

Siberian Husky

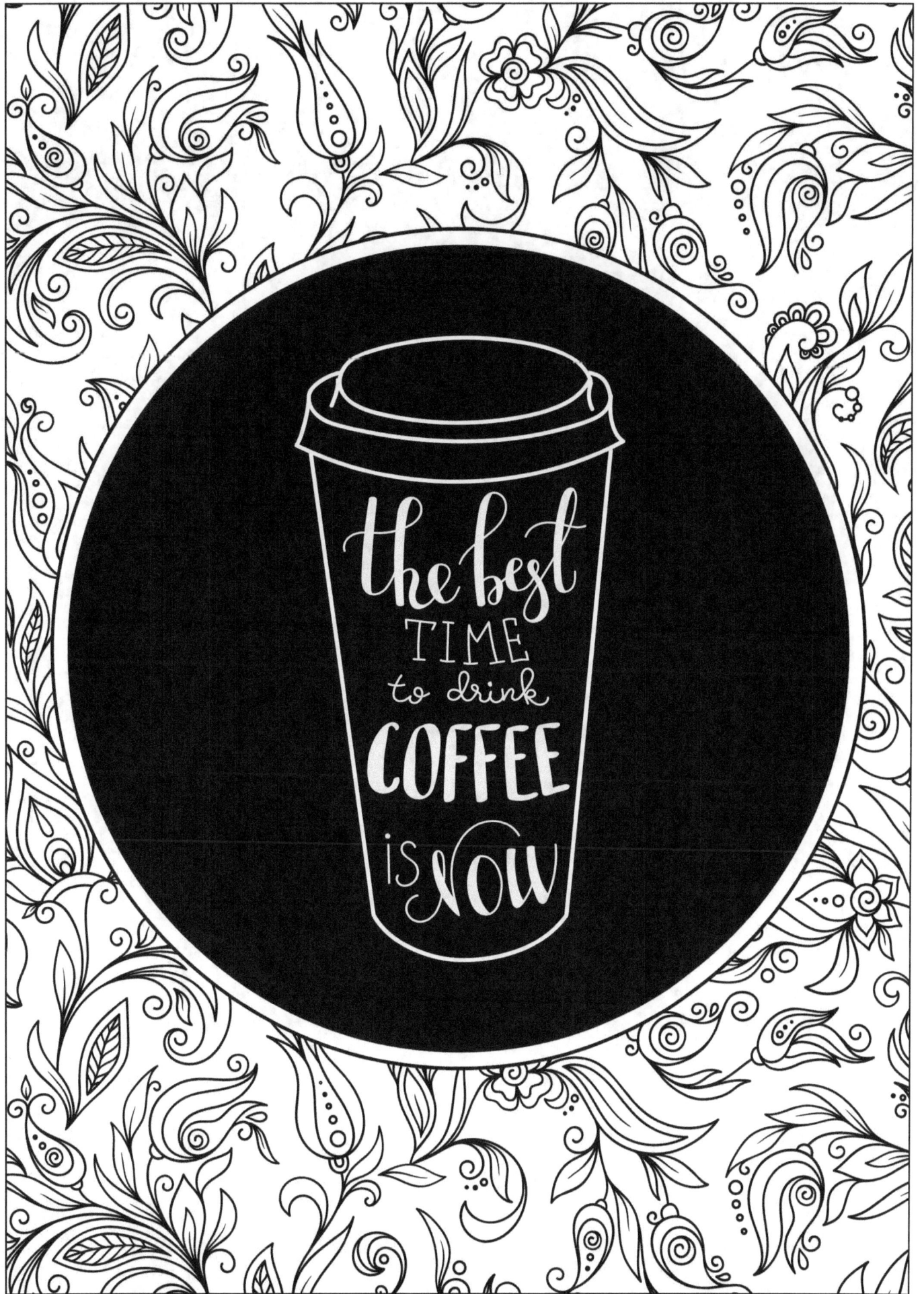

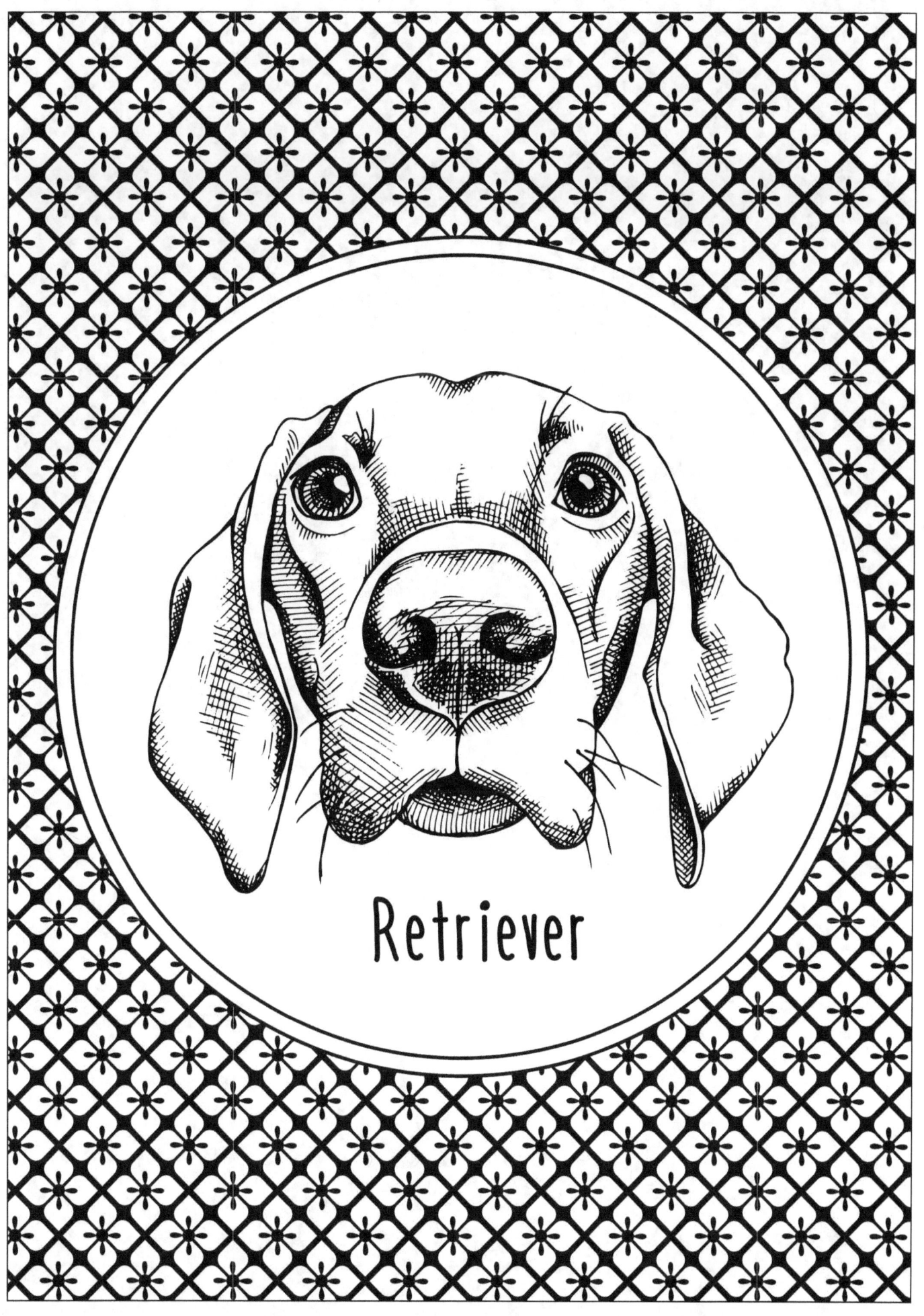

Retriever

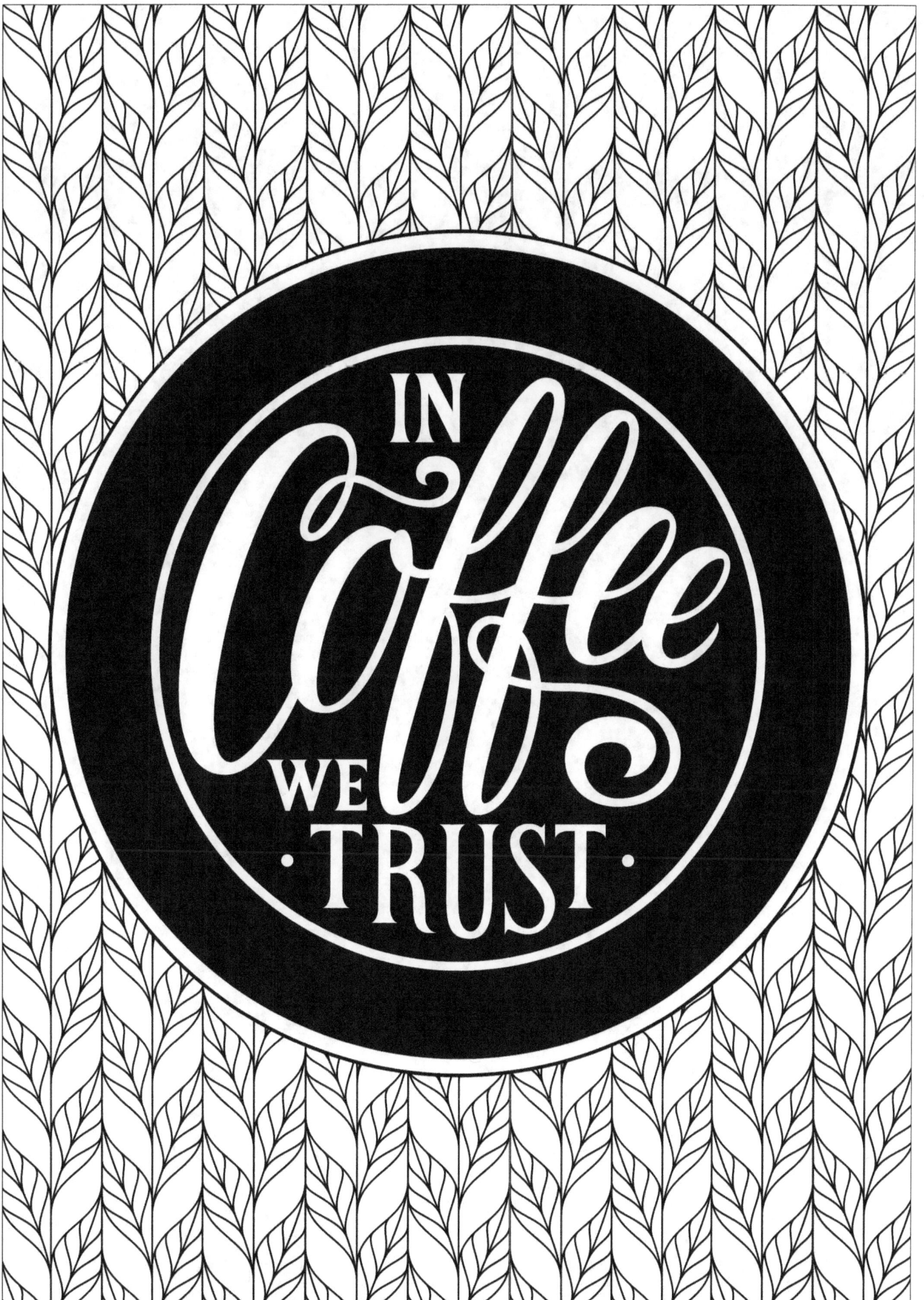

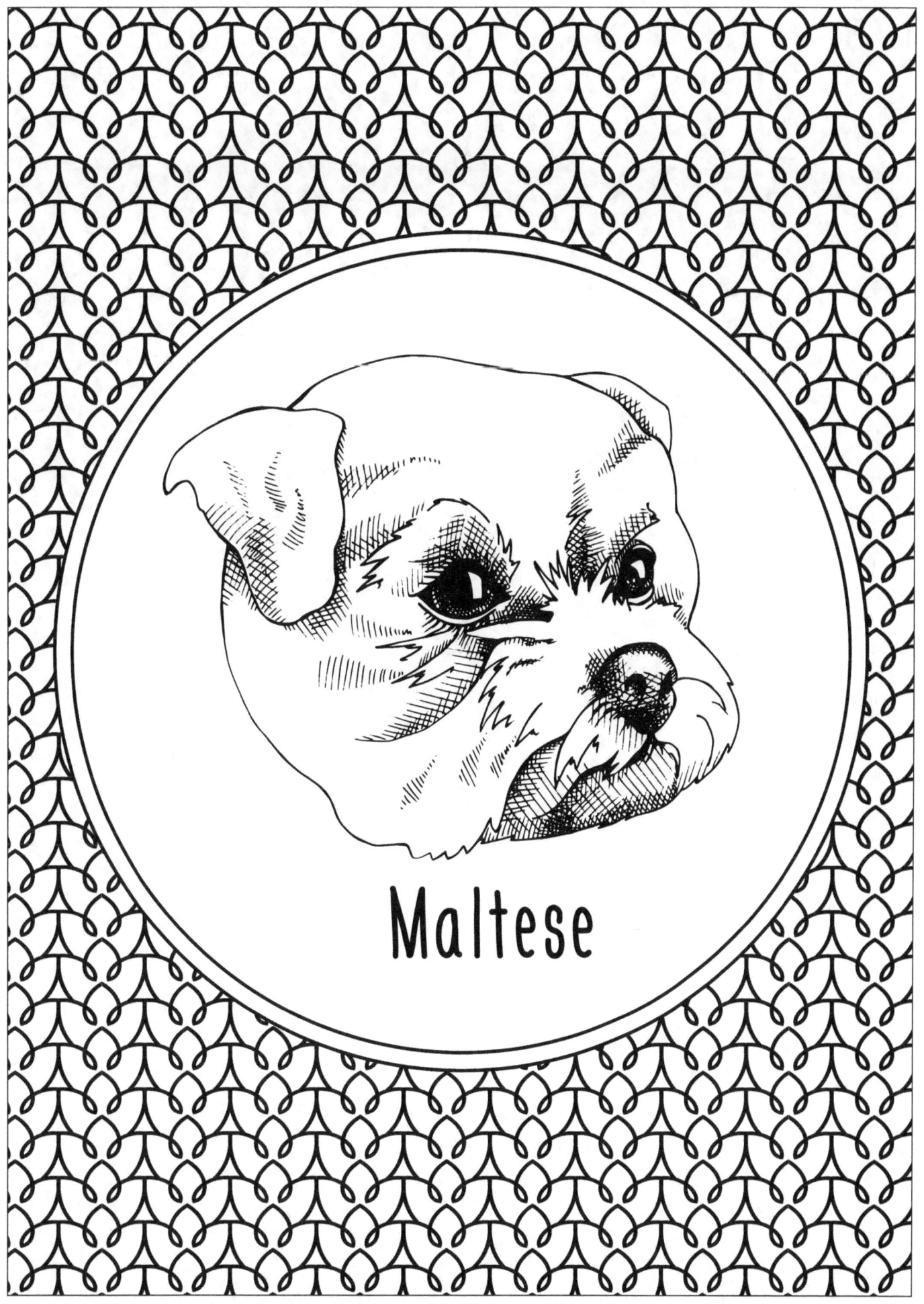

Maltese

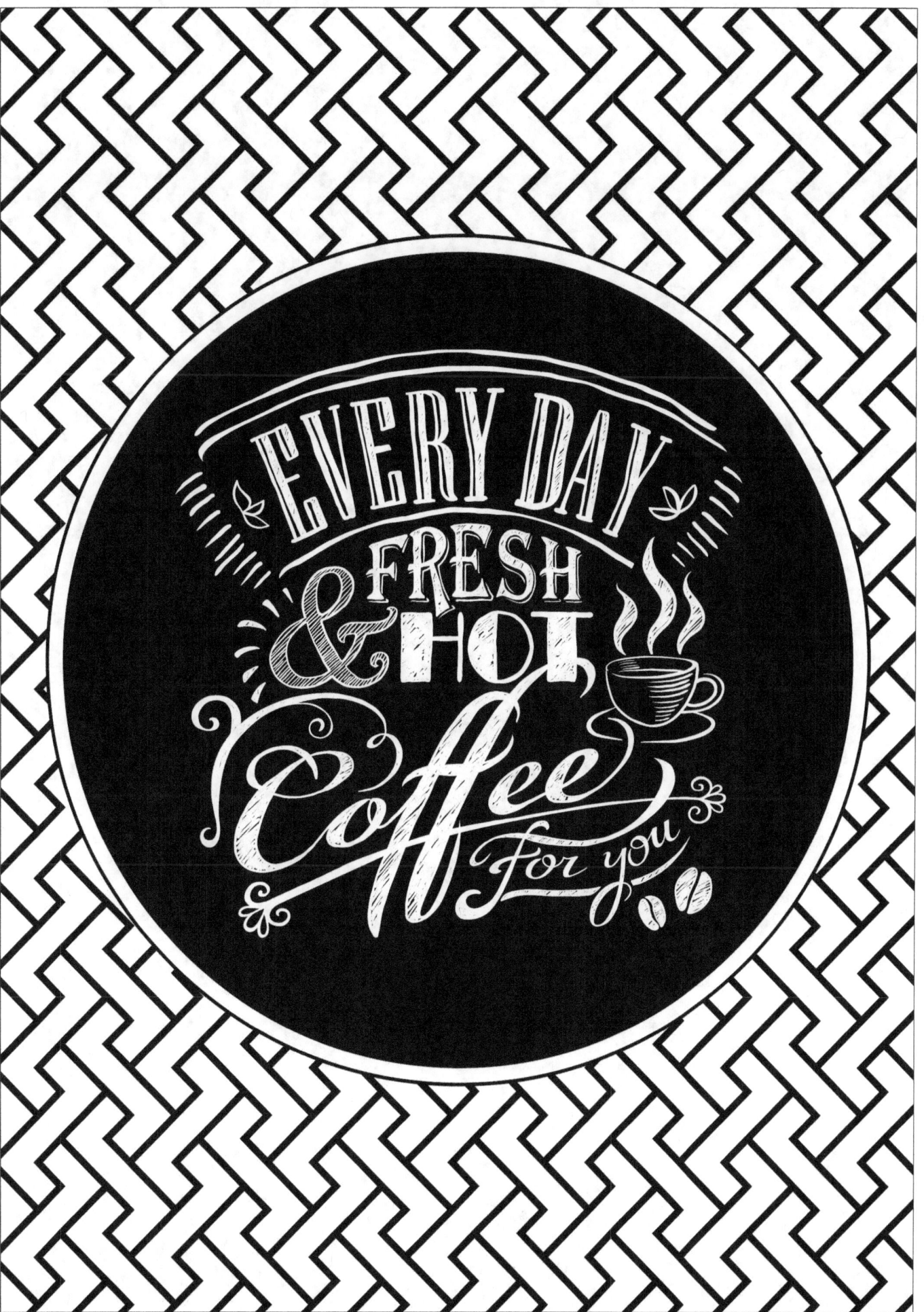

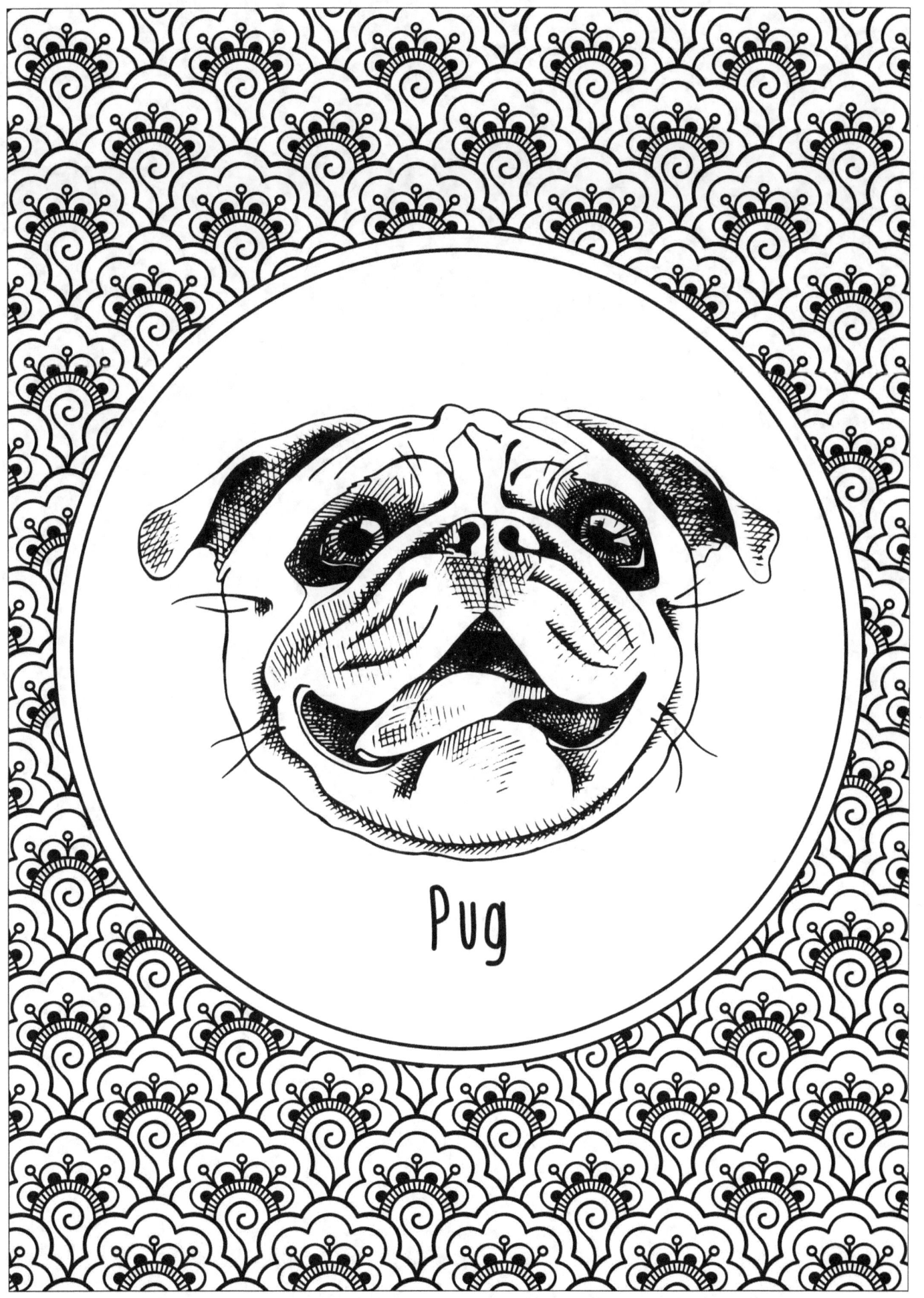

Pug

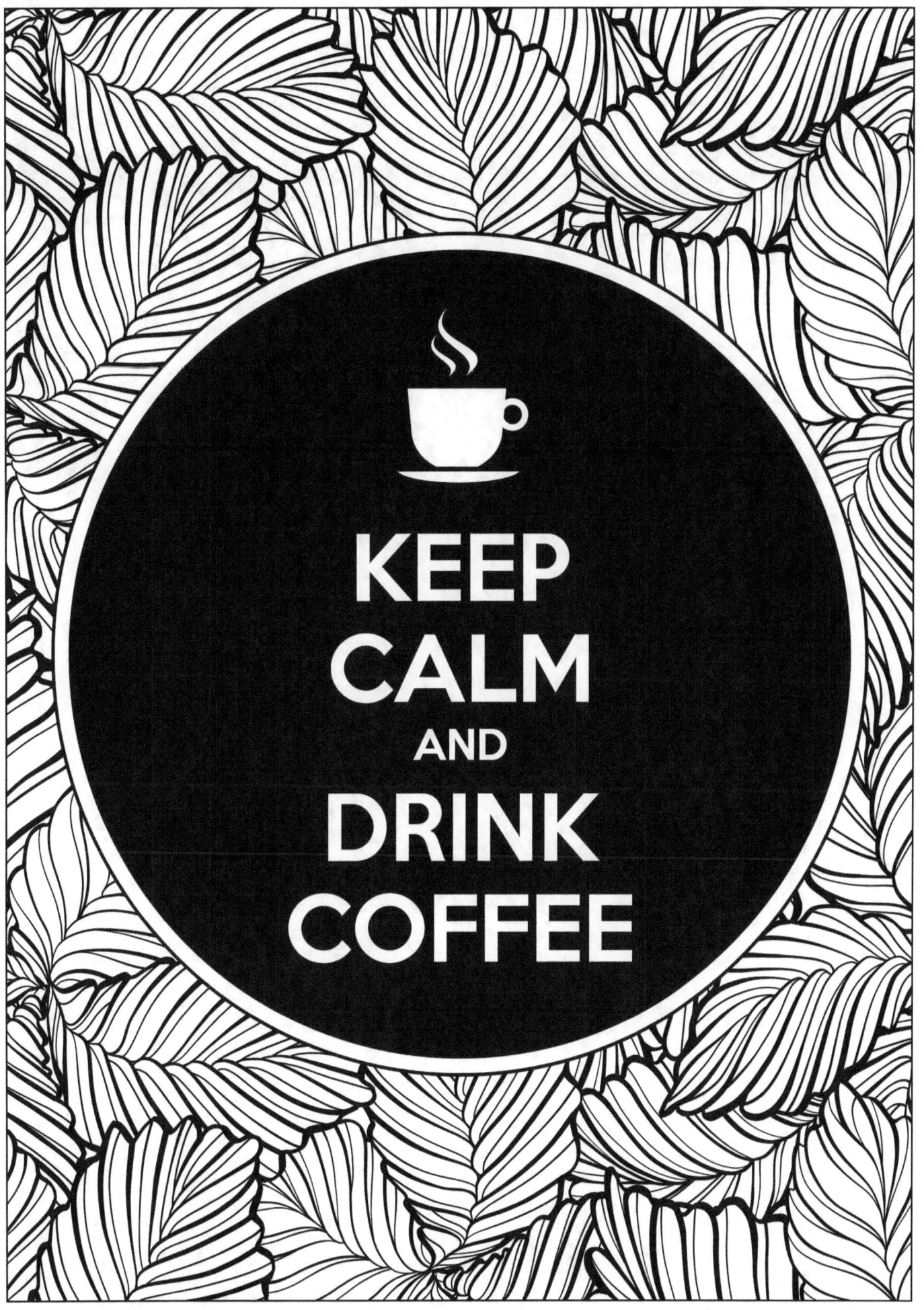

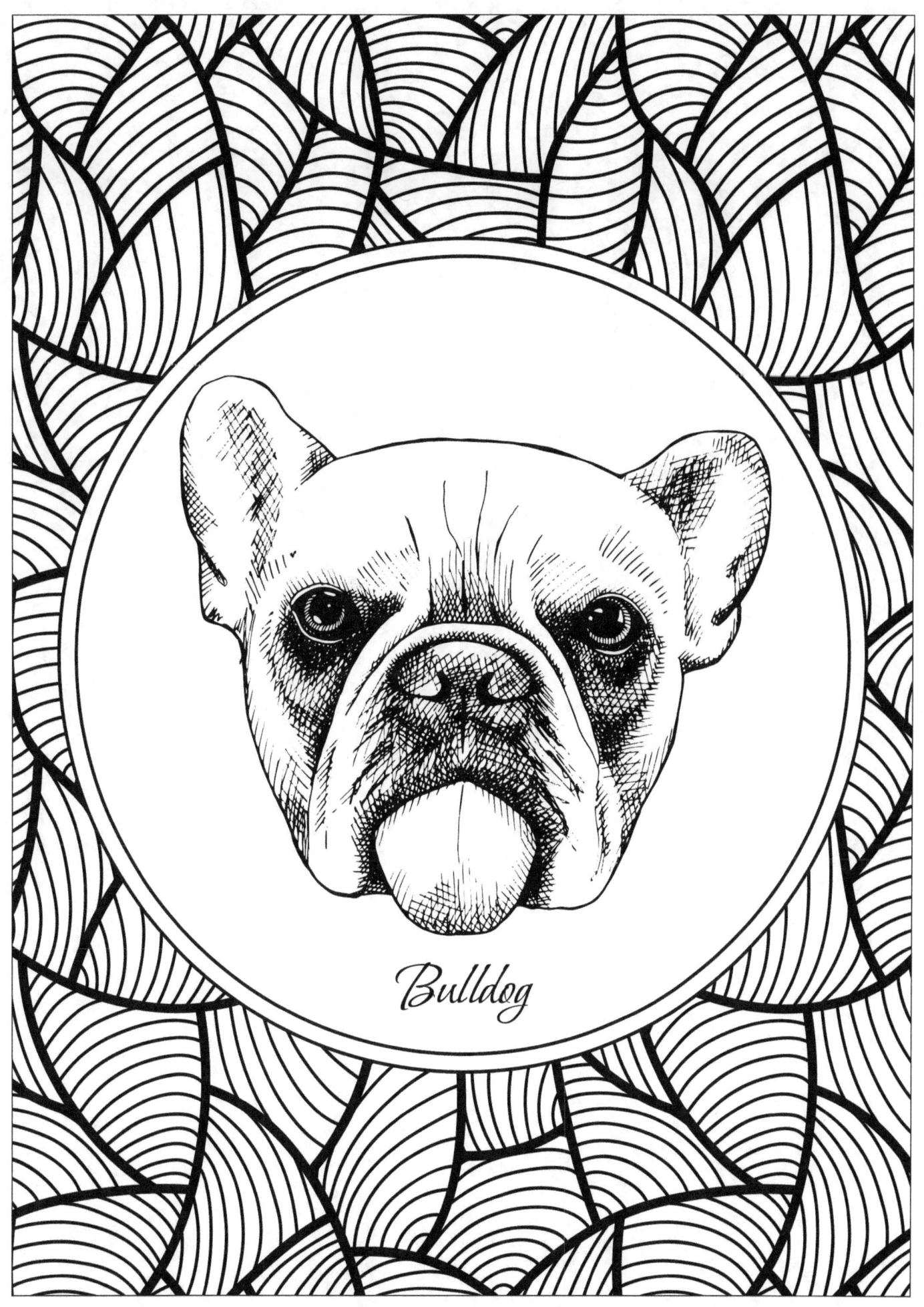

Bulldog

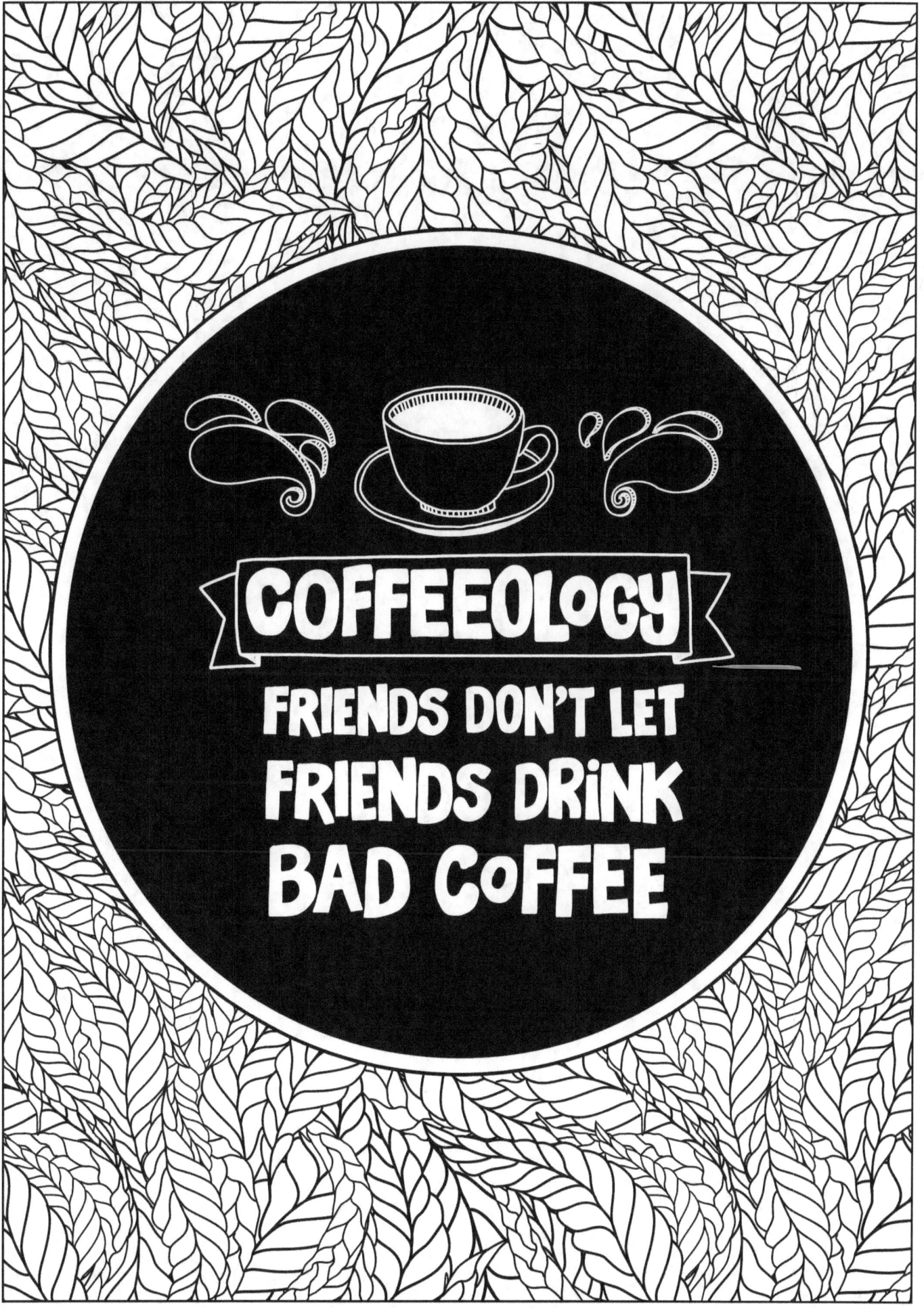

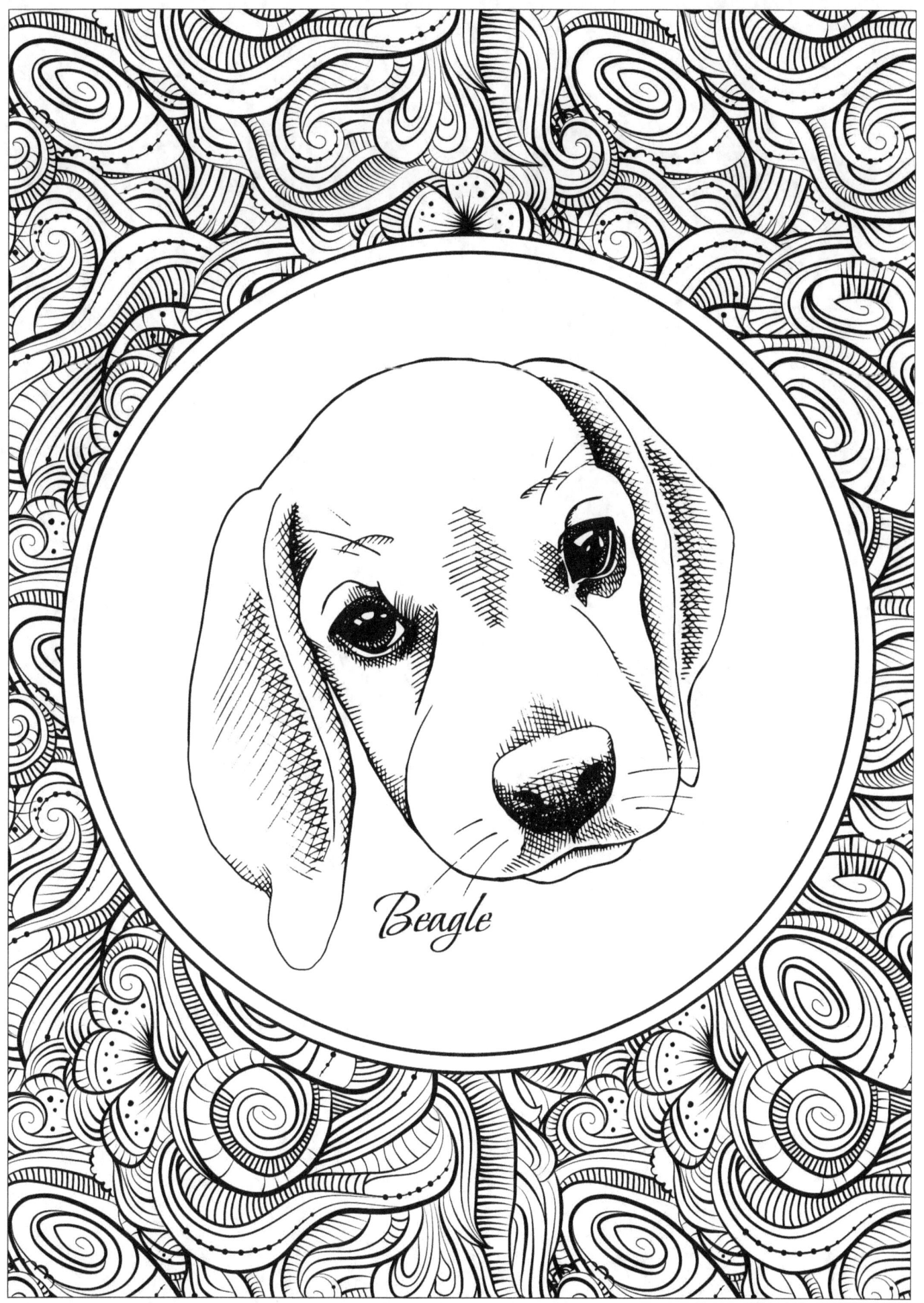

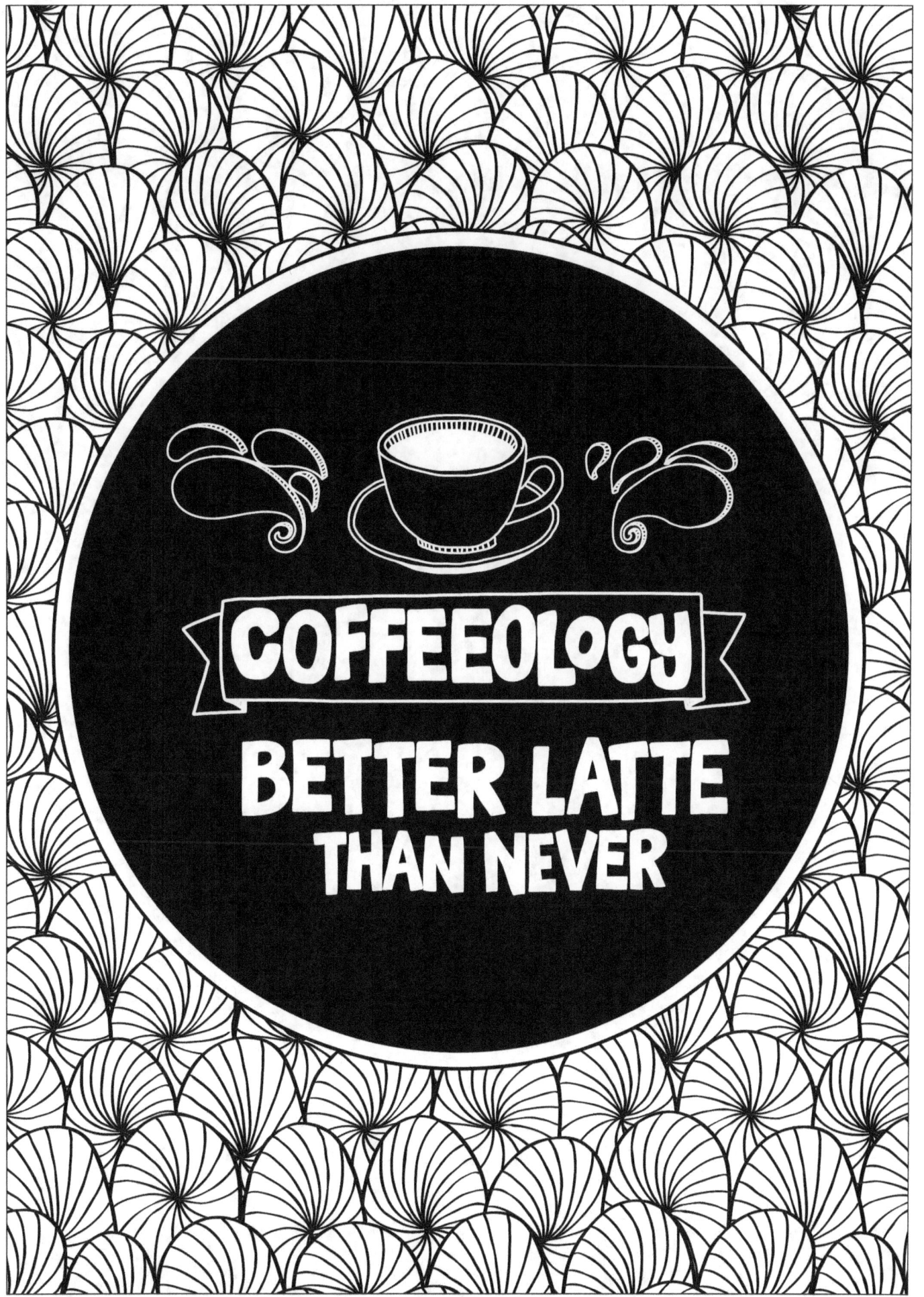

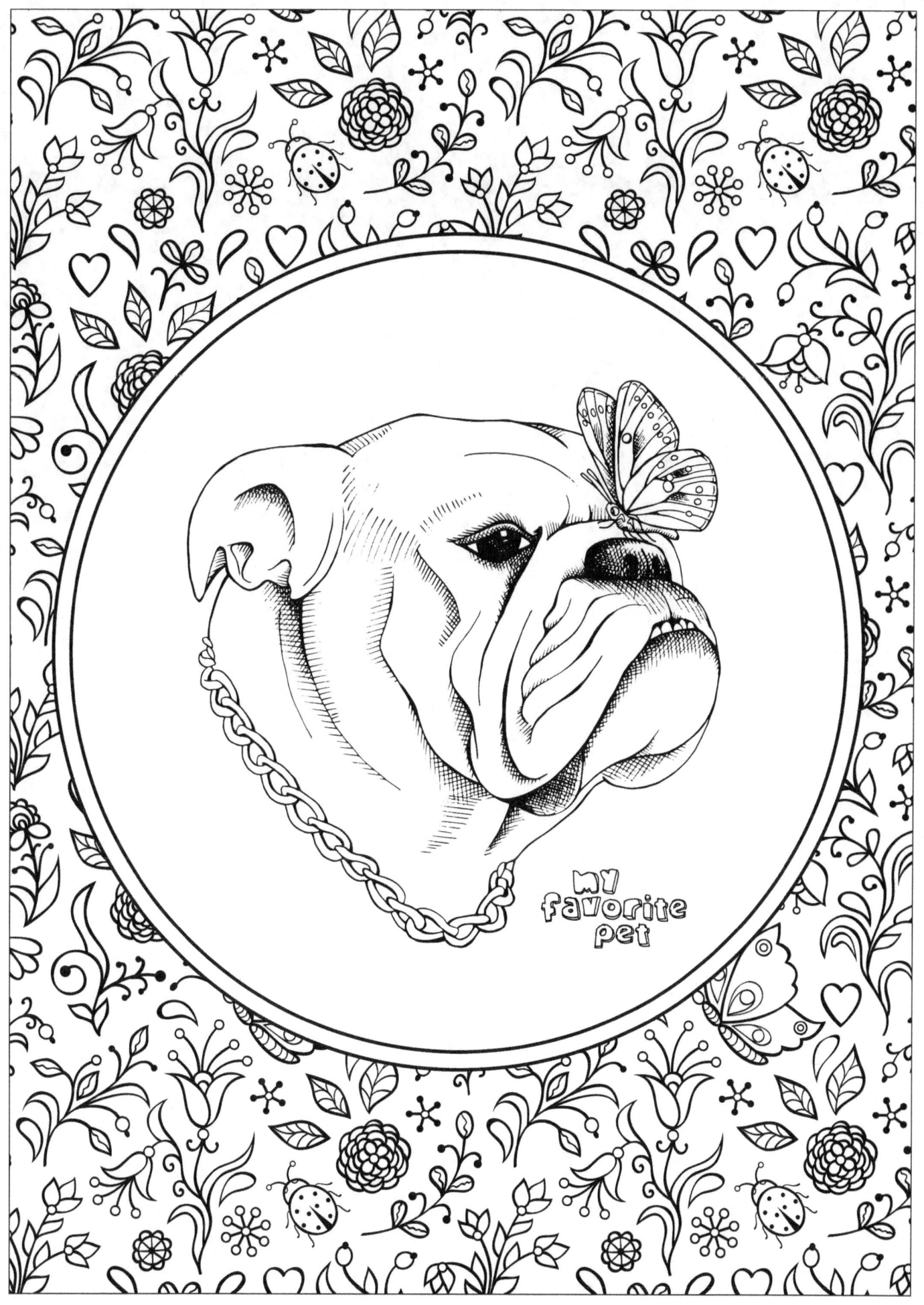

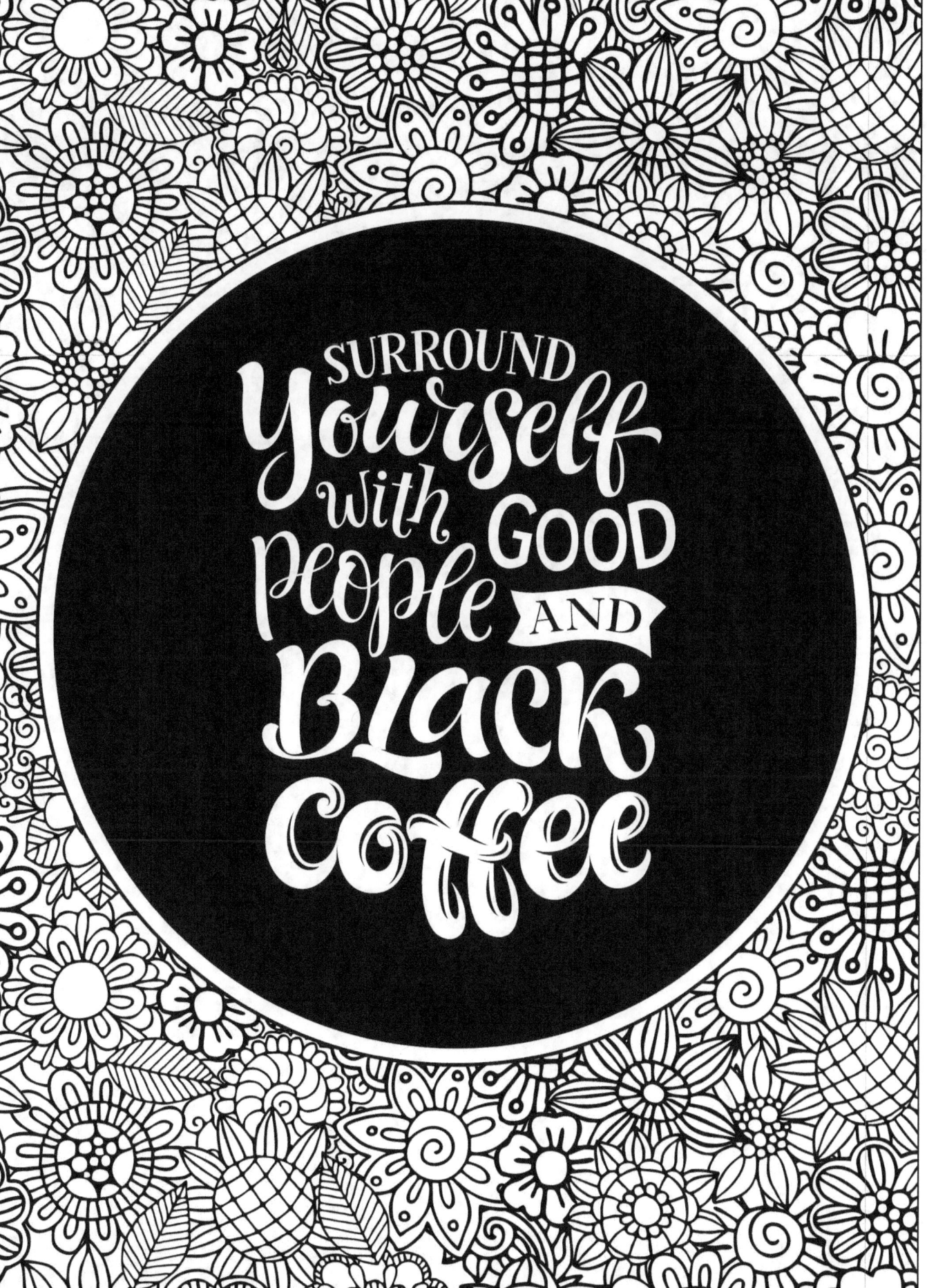

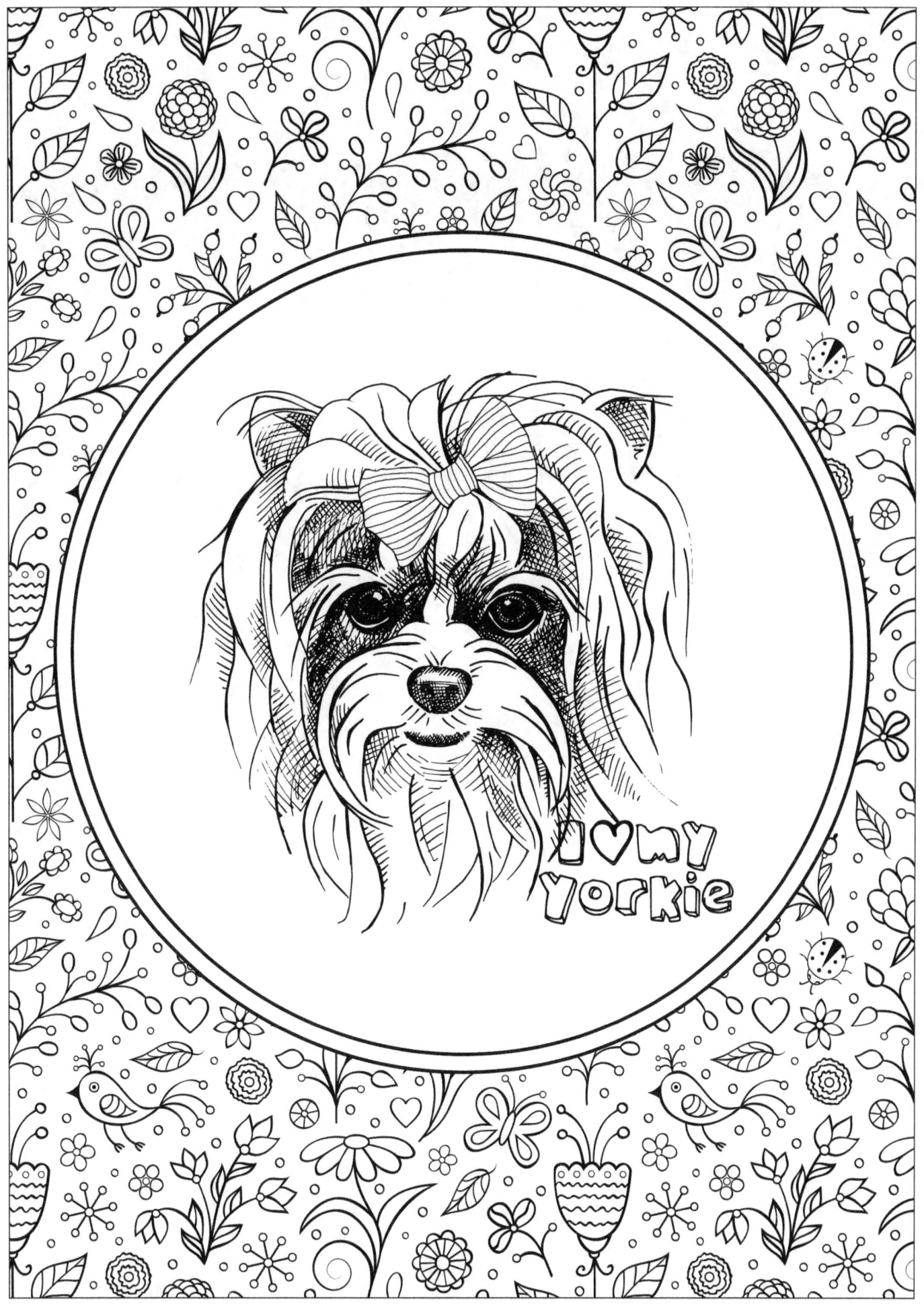

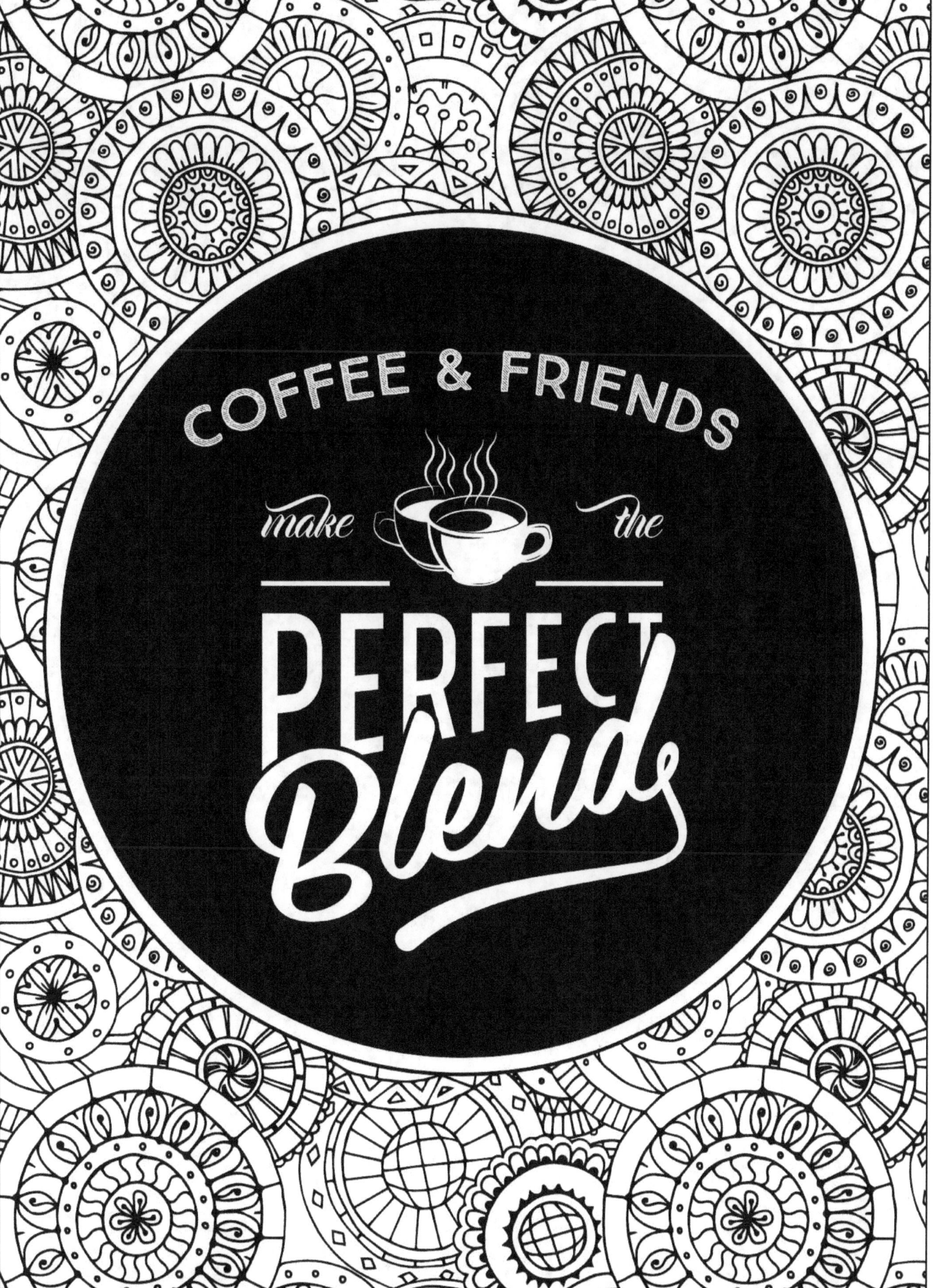

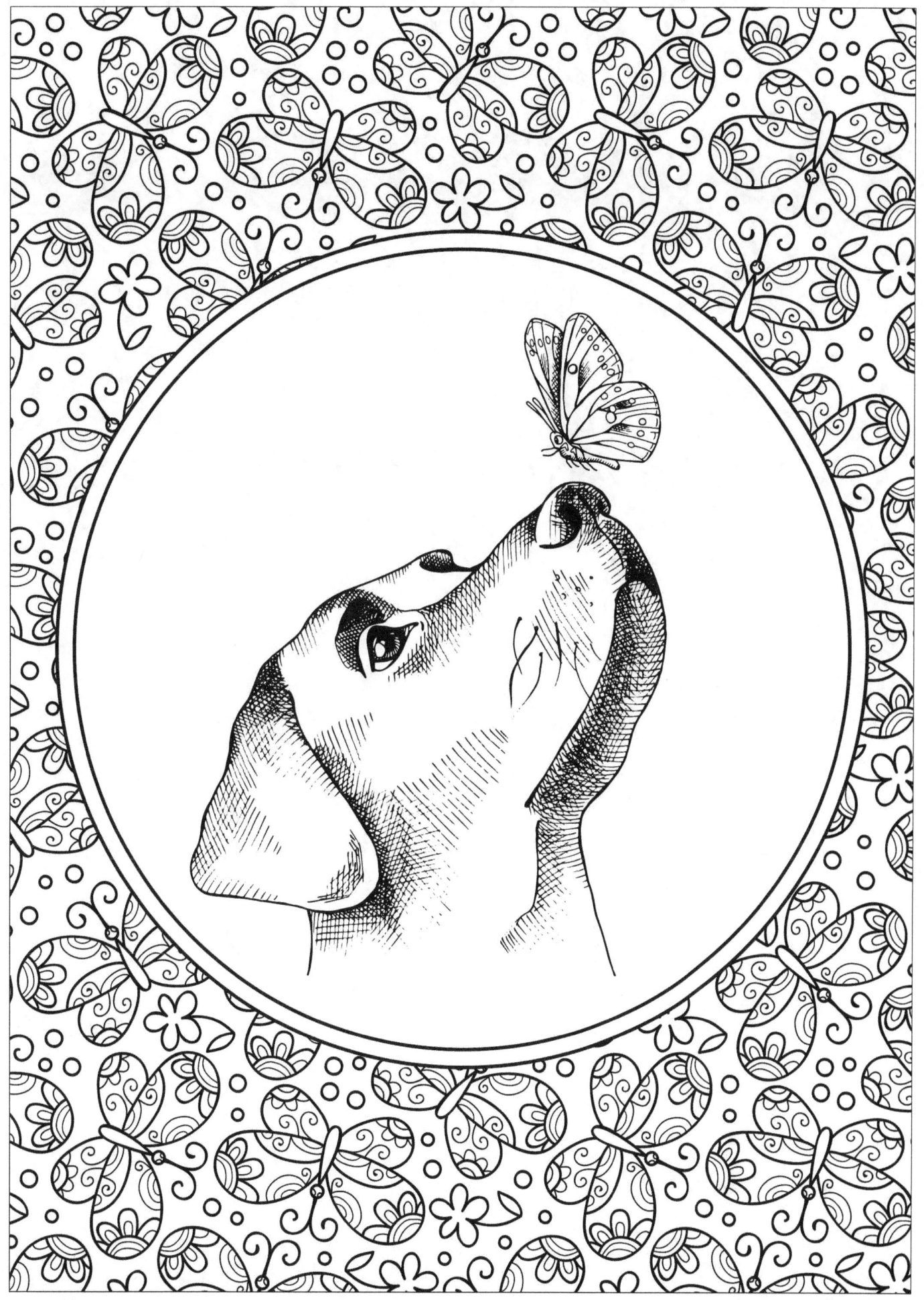

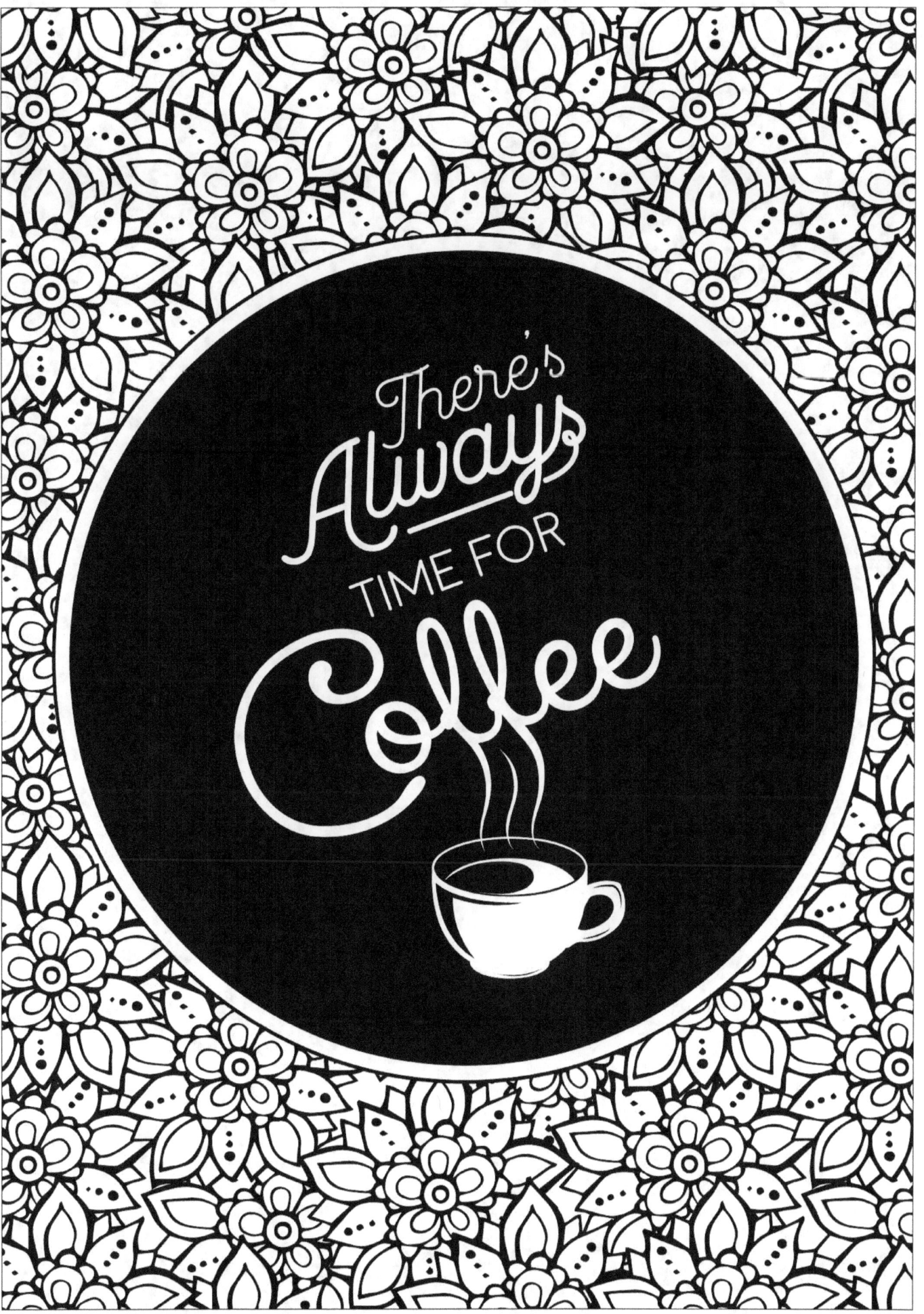

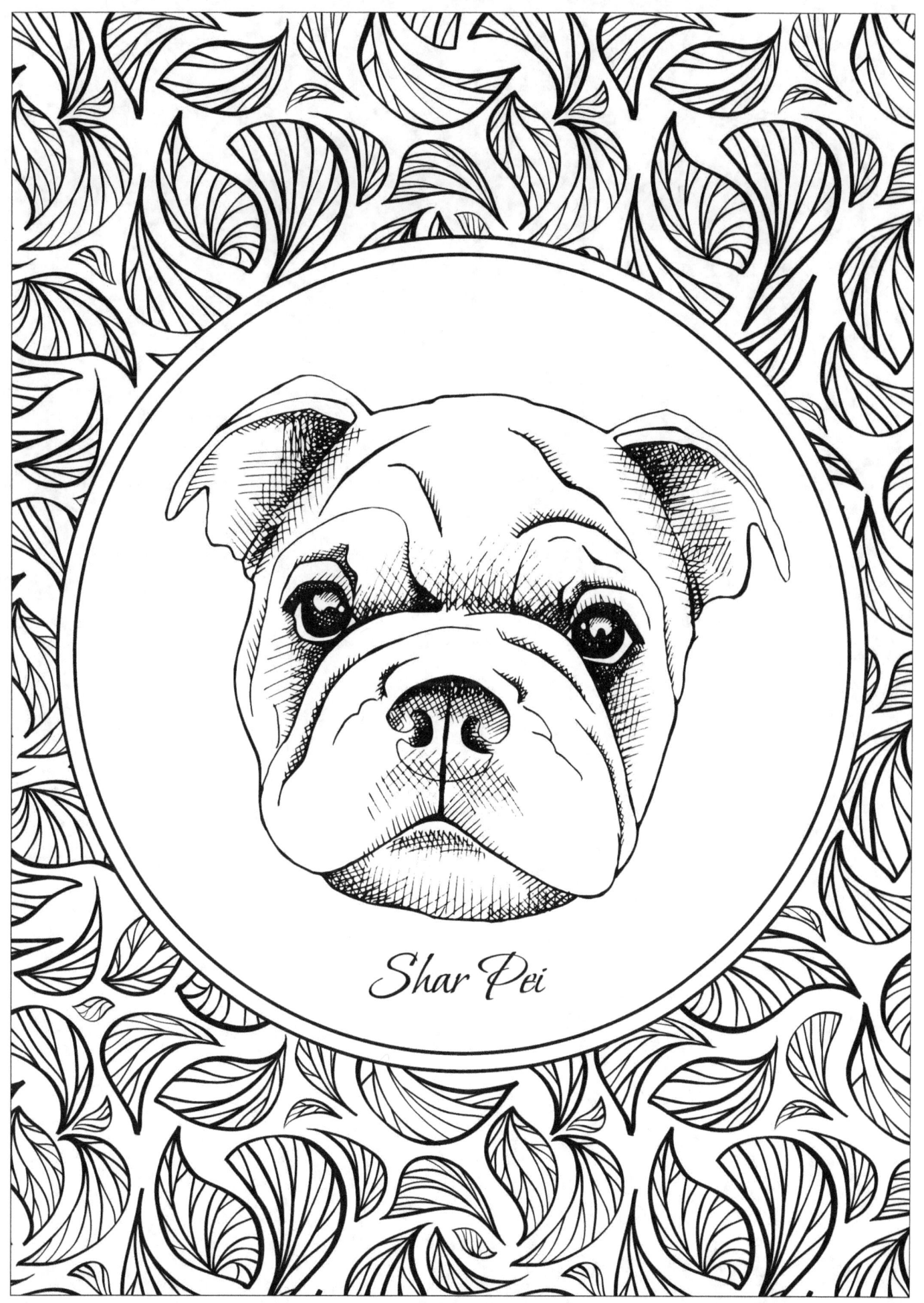

Shar Pei

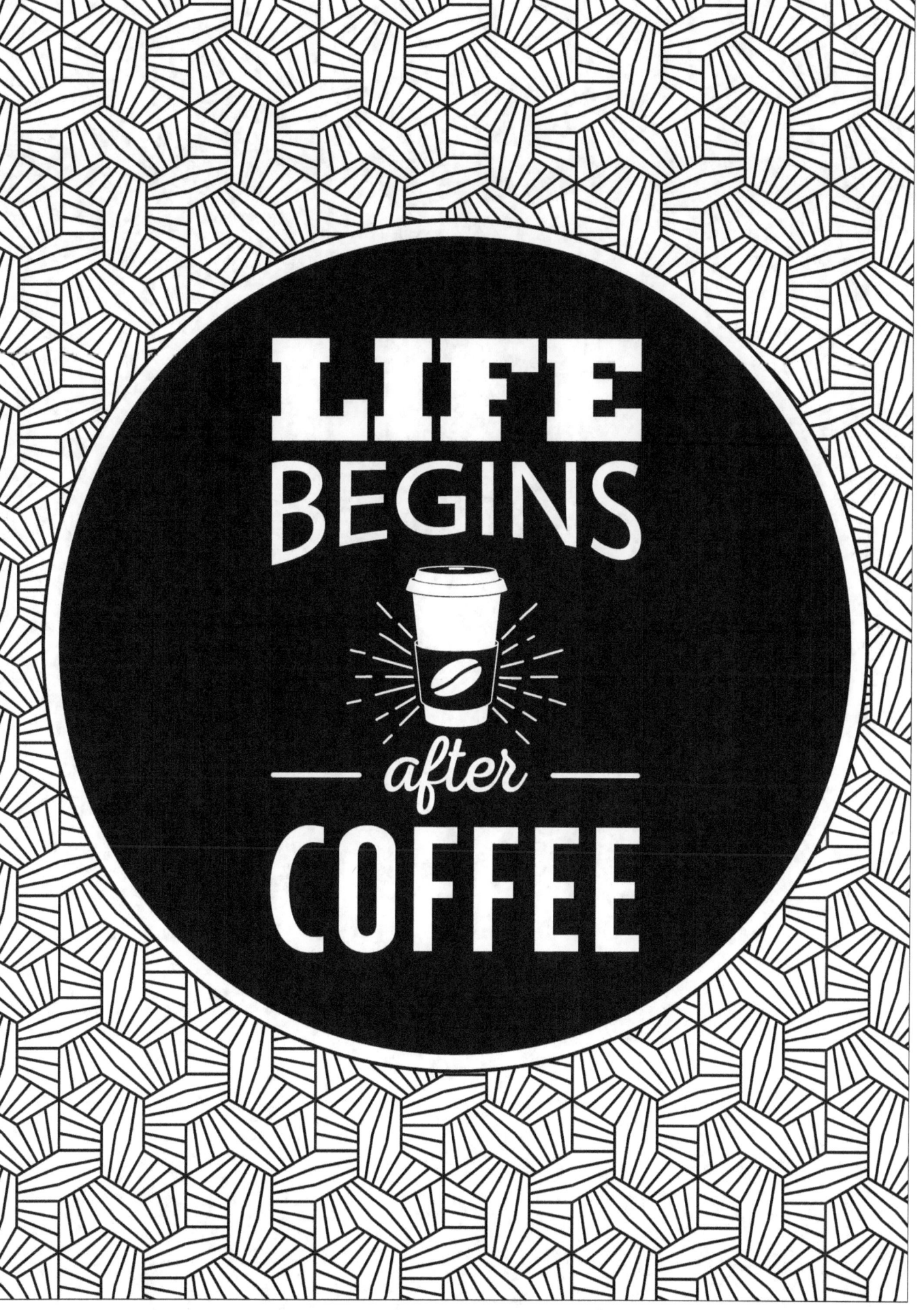

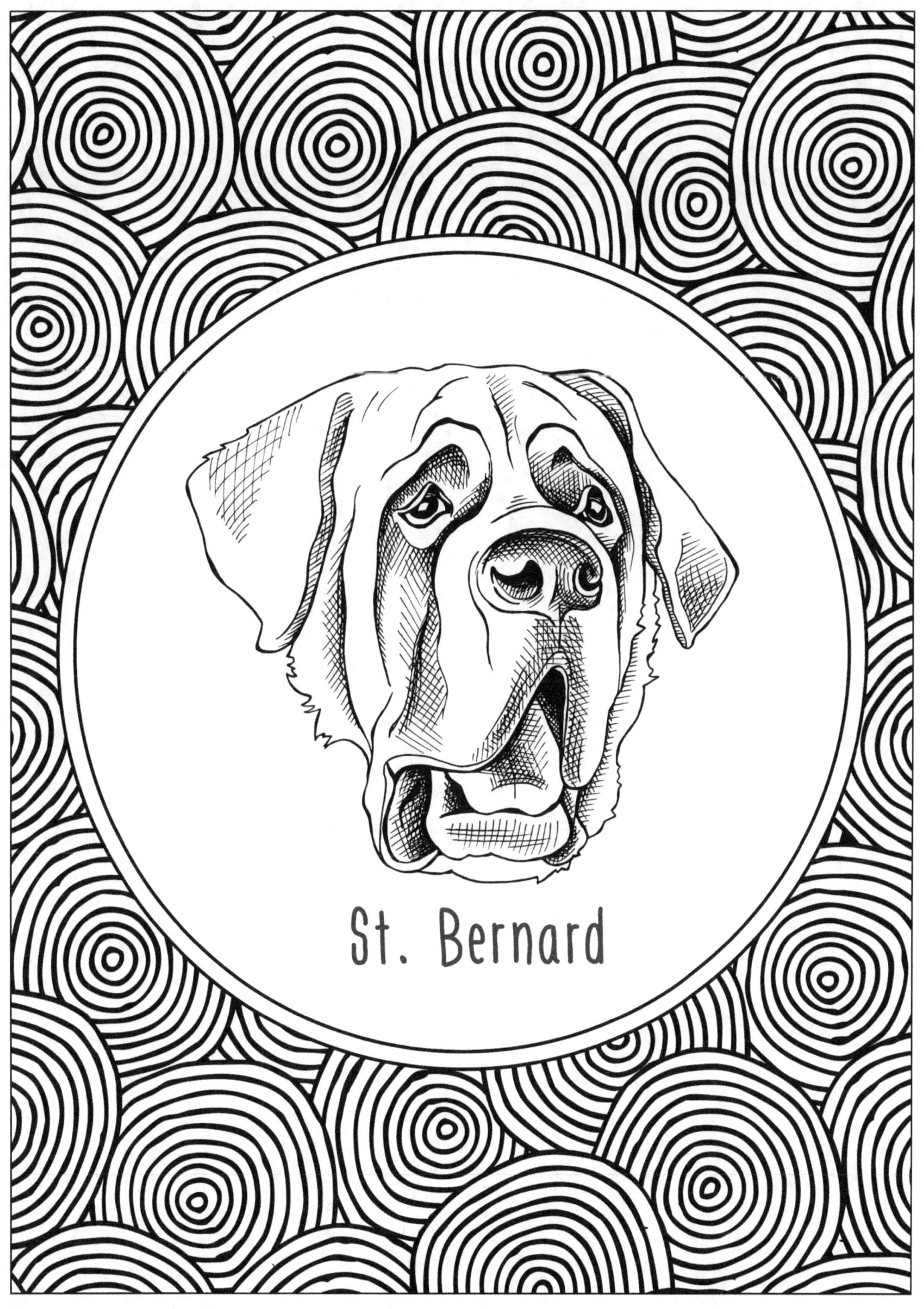

St. Bernard

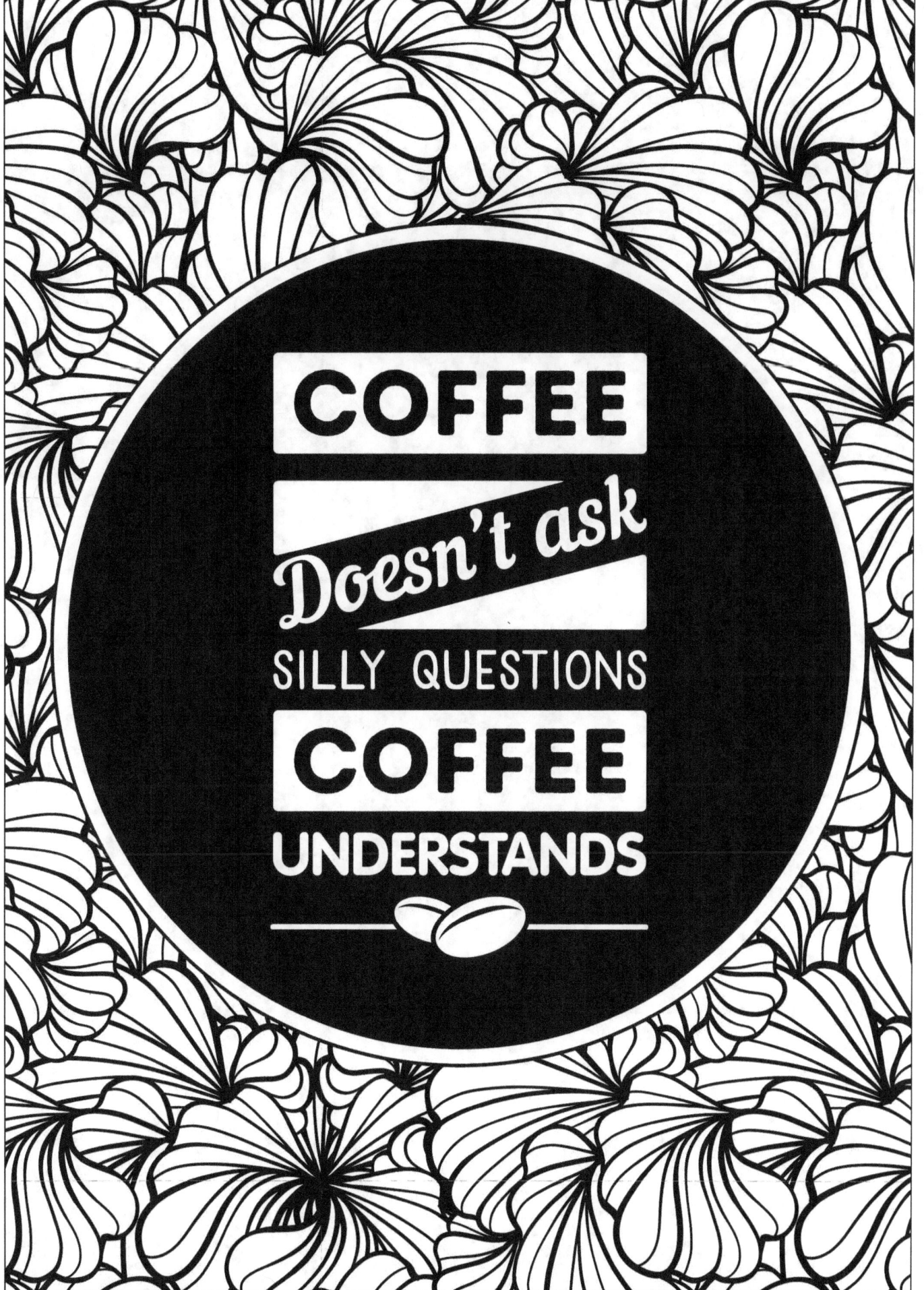

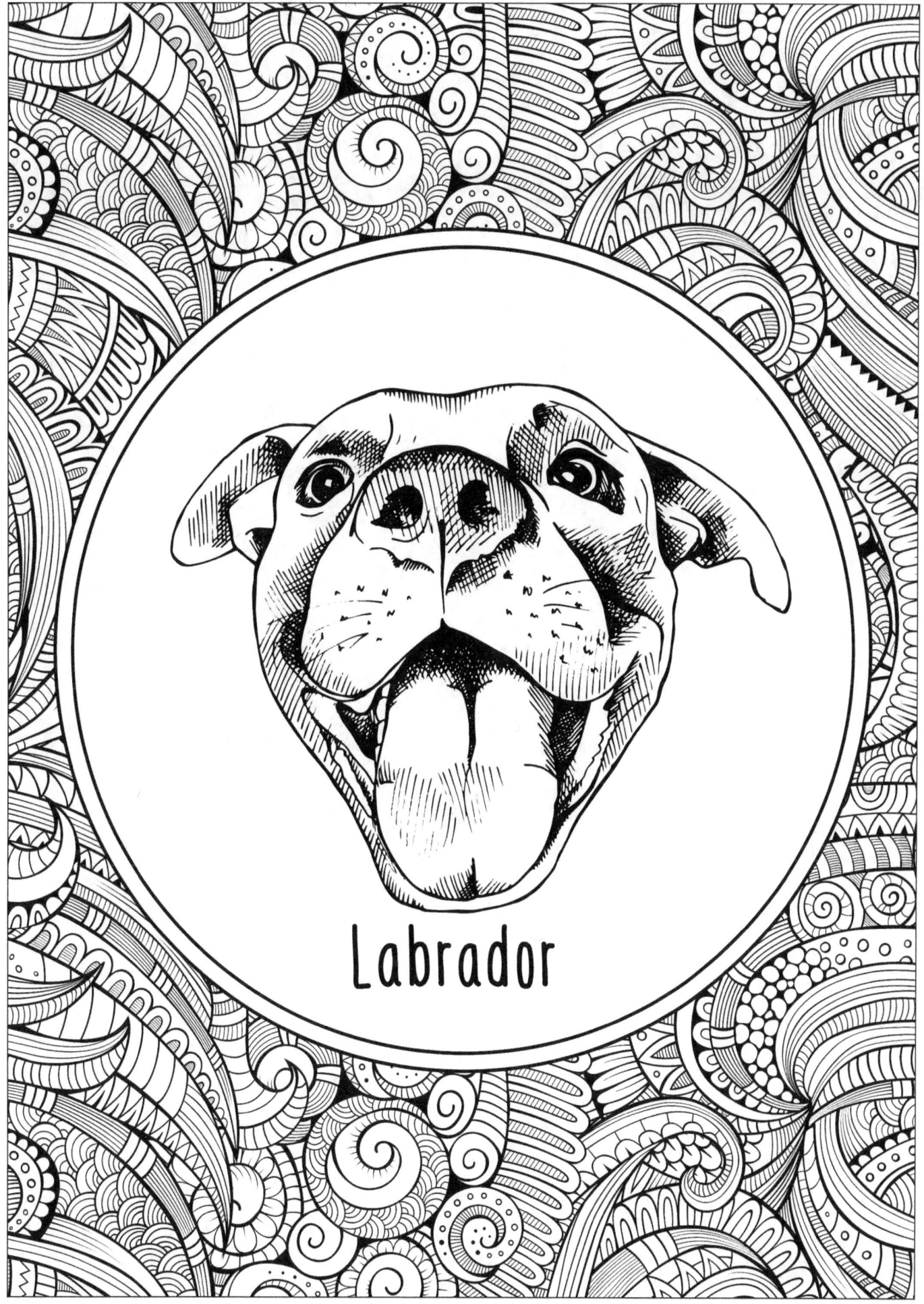

Labrador

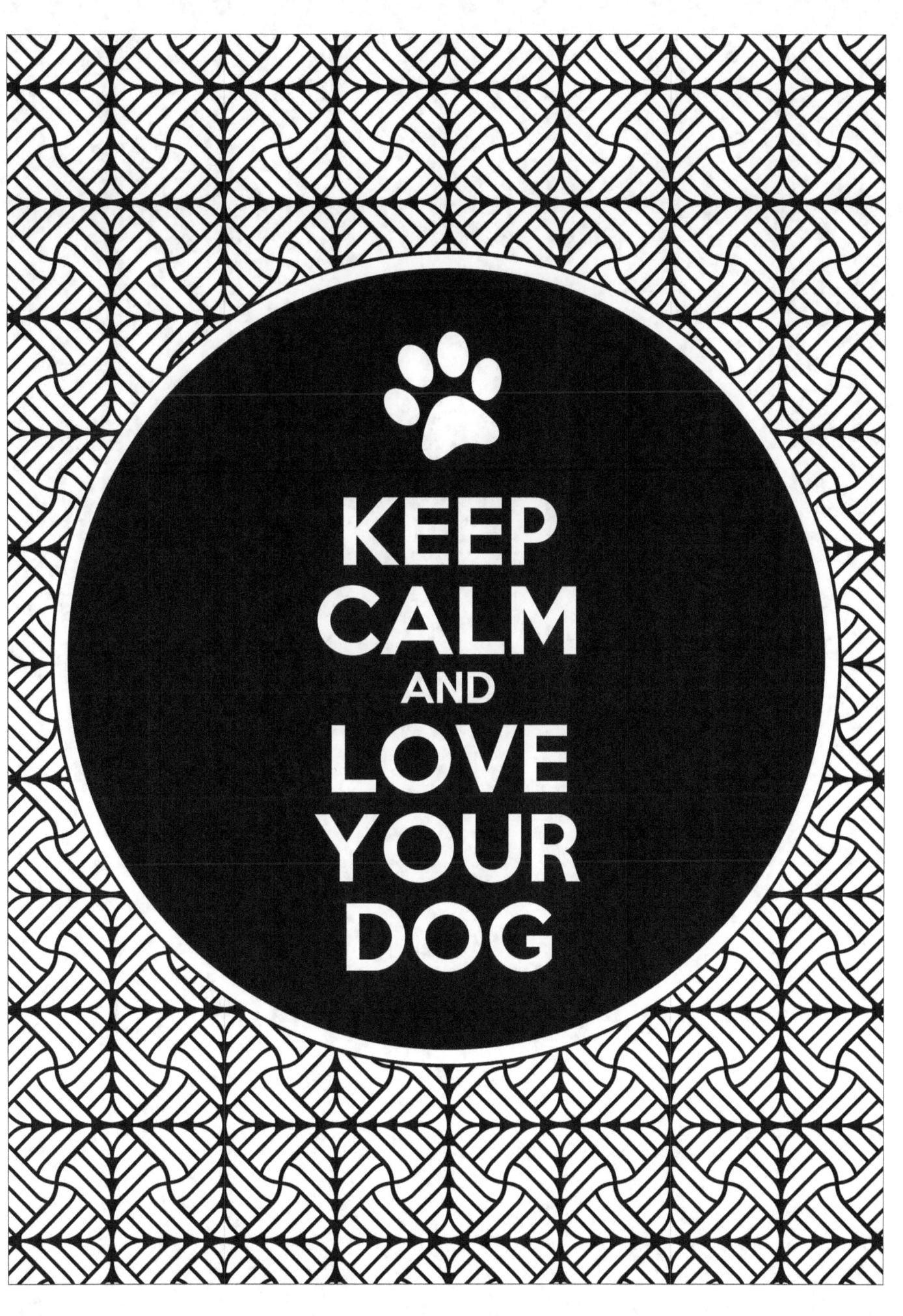

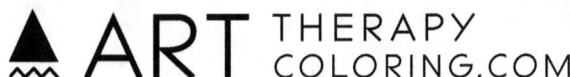

Drawings

Drawings

Drawings

Art Therapy Coloring Books

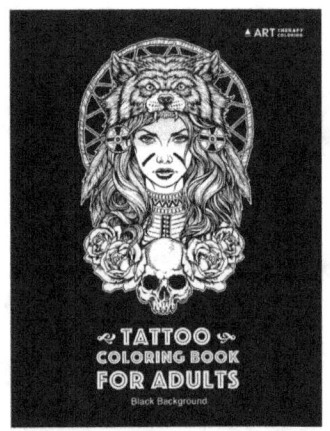

TATTOO COLORING BOOK FOR ADULTS
Black Background

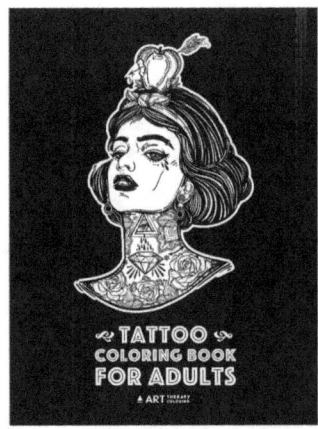

TATTOO COLORING BOOK FOR ADULTS

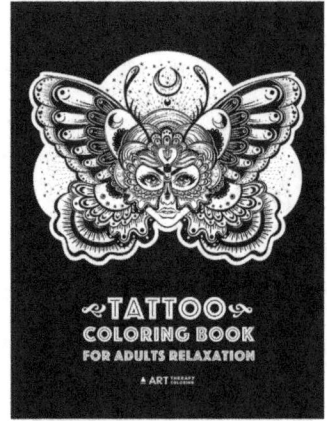

TATTOO COLORING BOOK FOR ADULTS RELAXATION

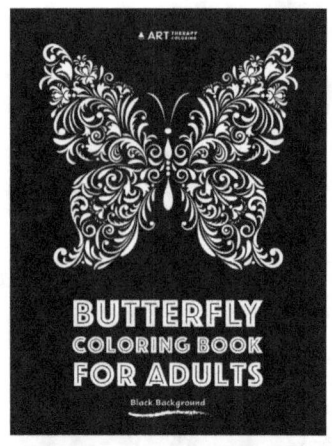

BUTTERFLY COLORING BOOK FOR ADULTS
Black Background

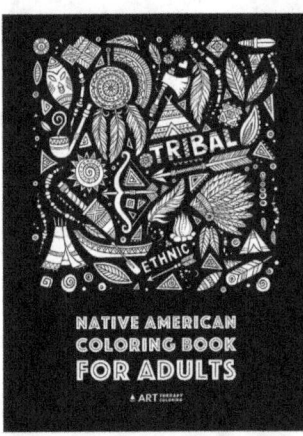

NATIVE AMERICAN COLORING BOOK FOR ADULTS

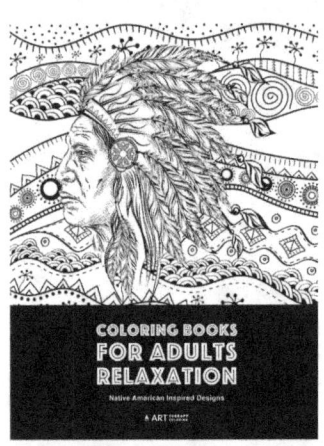

COLORING BOOKS FOR ADULTS RELAXATION
Native American Inspired Designs

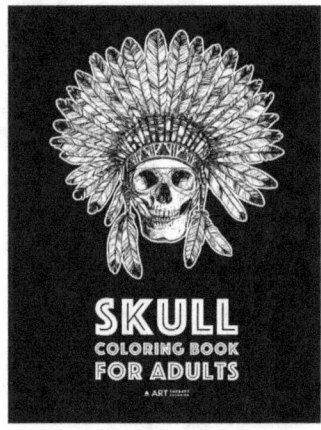

SKULL COLORING BOOK FOR ADULTS

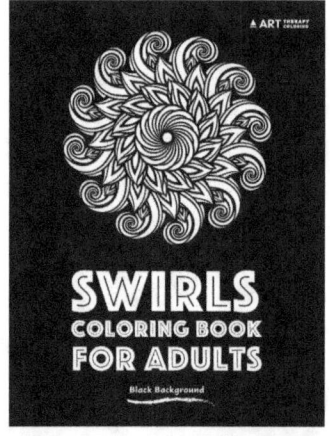

SWIRLS COLORING BOOK FOR ADULTS
Black Background

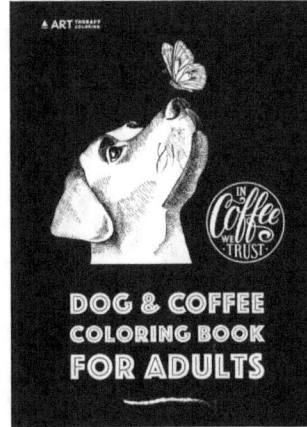

DOG & COFFEE COLORING BOOK FOR ADULTS

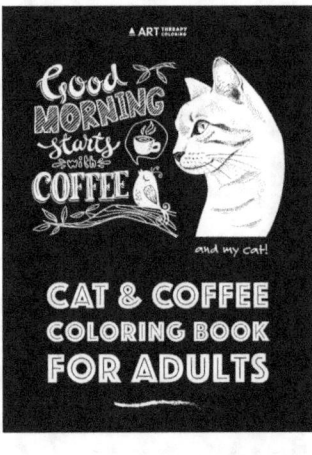

CAT & COFFEE COLORING BOOK FOR ADULTS

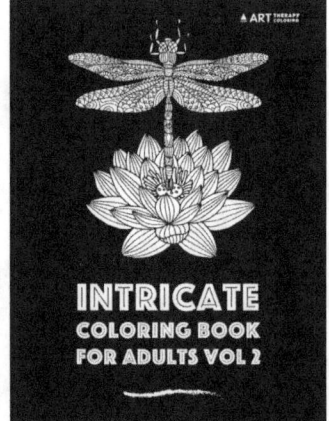

INTRICATE COLORING BOOK FOR ADULTS VOL 2

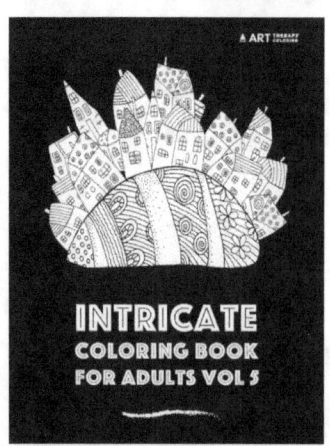

INTRICATE COLORING BOOK FOR ADULTS VOL 5

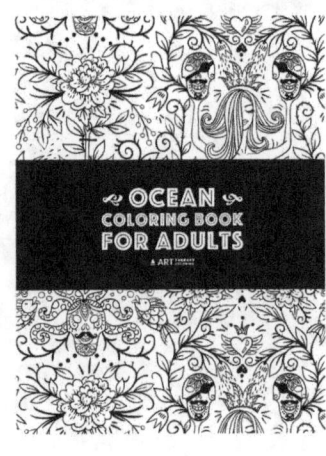

OCEAN COLORING BOOK FOR ADULTS

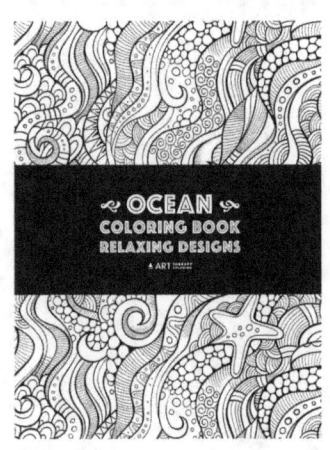

OCEAN COLORING BOOK RELAXING DESIGNS

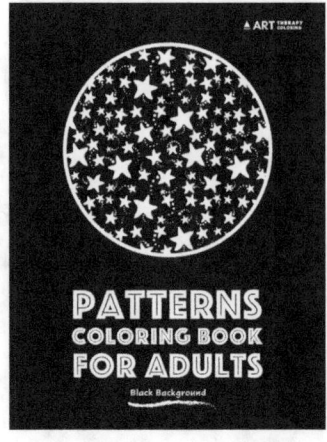

PATTERNS COLORING BOOK FOR ADULTS
Black Background

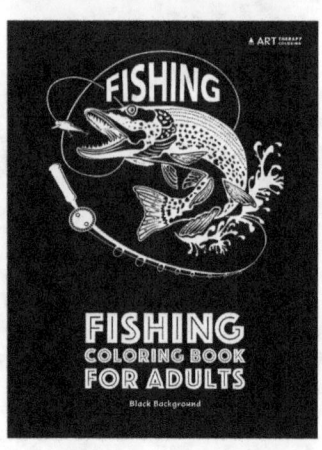

FISHING COLORING BOOK FOR ADULTS
Black Background

Art Therapy Coloring Books

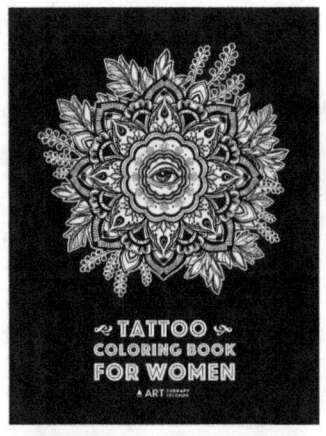

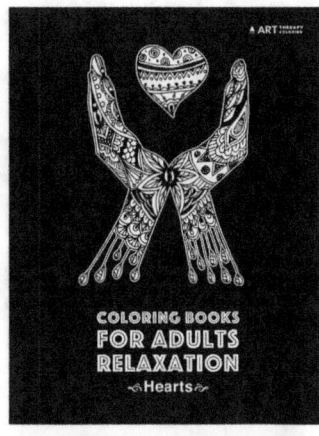

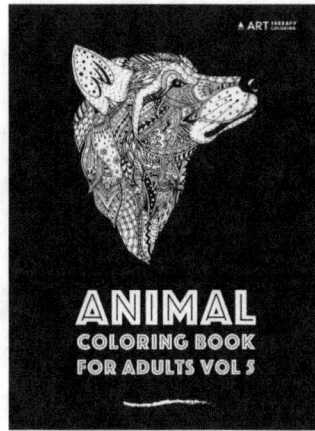

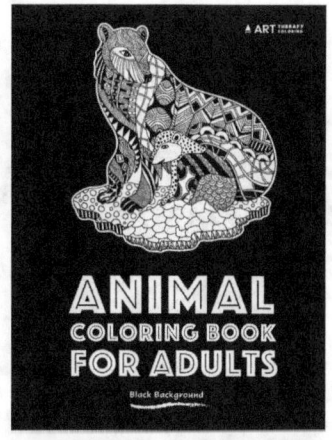

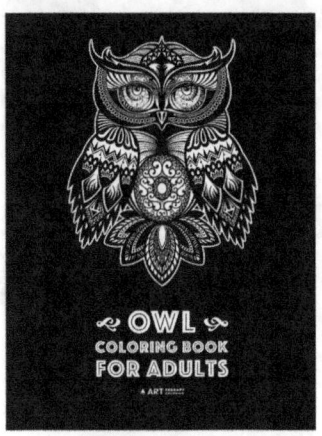

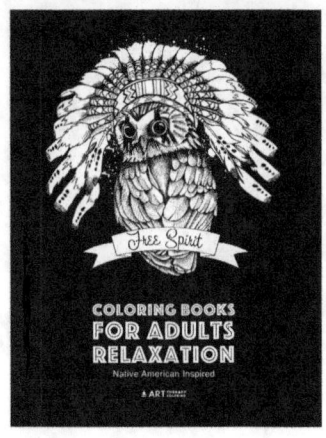

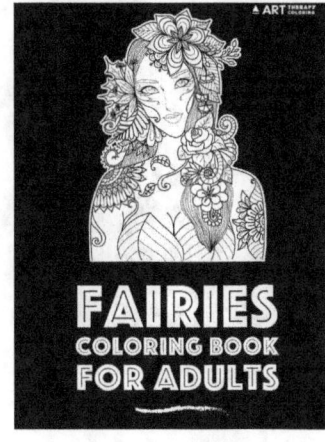

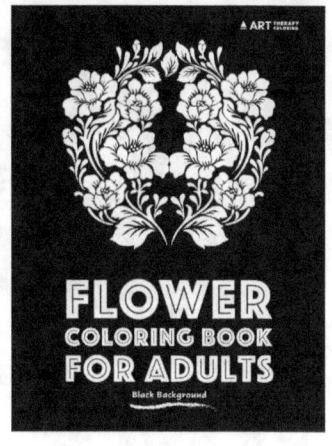

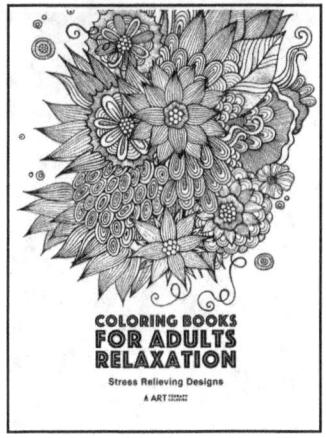

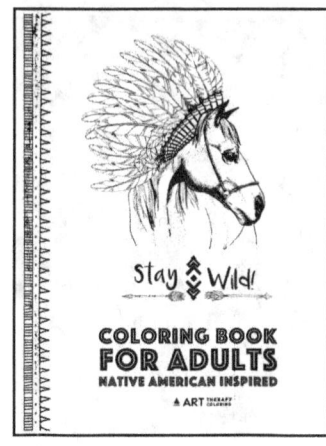

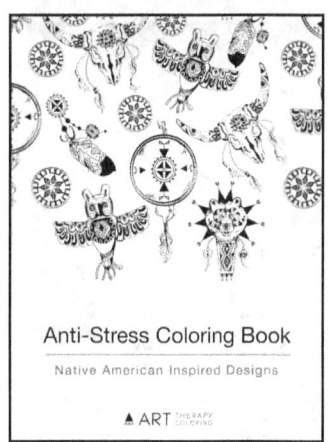

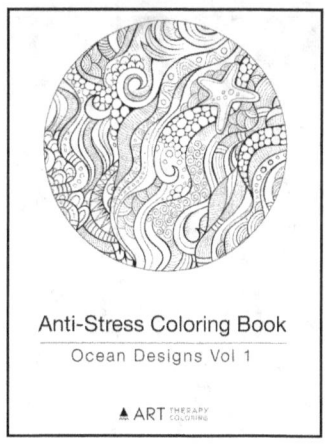

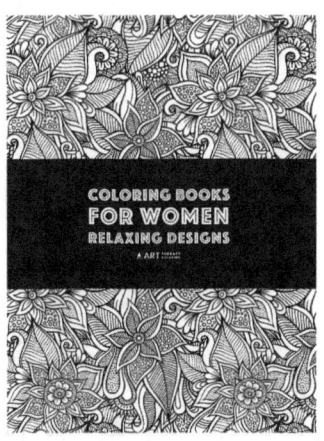

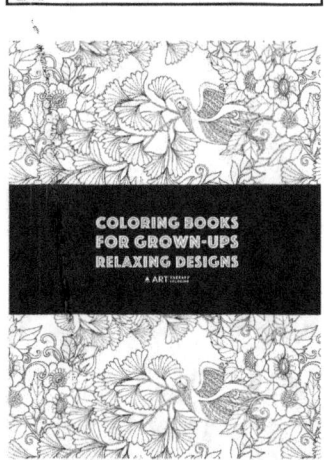

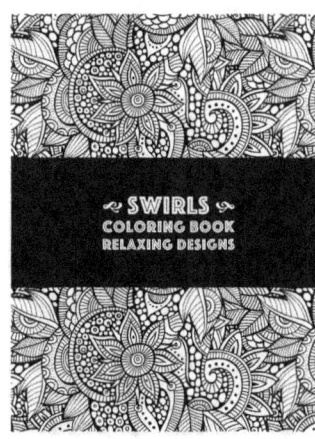

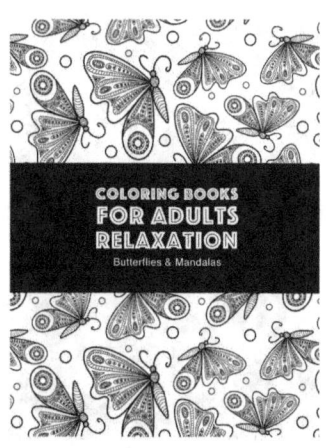

Art Therapy Coloring Books

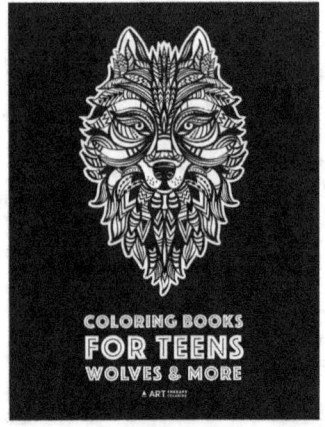

COLORING BOOKS
FOR TEENS
WOLVES & MORE

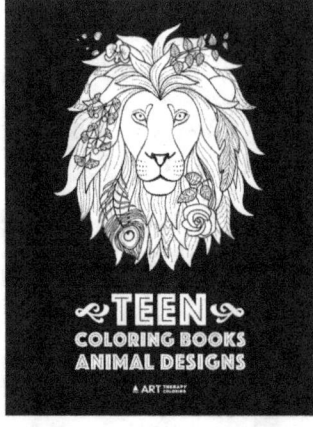

TEEN
COLORING BOOKS
ANIMAL DESIGNS

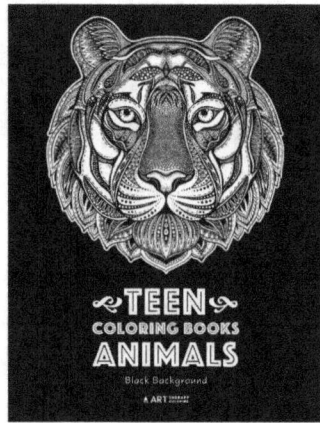

TEEN
COLORING BOOKS
ANIMALS
Black Background

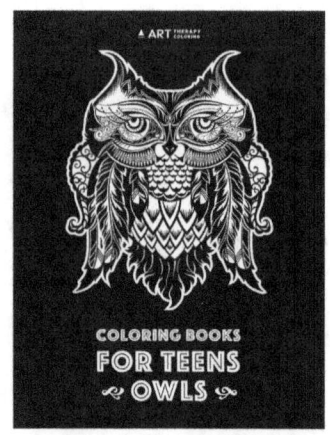

COLORING BOOKS
FOR TEENS
OWLS

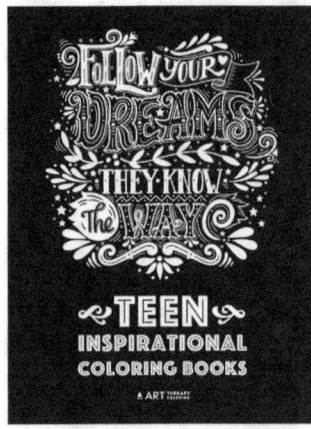

TEEN
INSPIRATIONAL
COLORING BOOKS

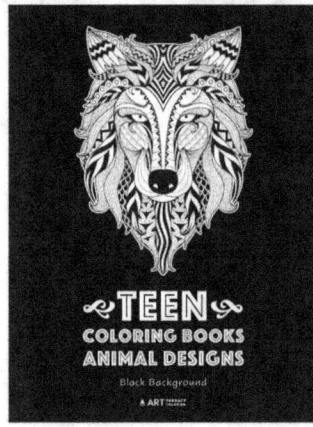

TEEN
COLORING BOOKS
ANIMAL DESIGNS
Black Background

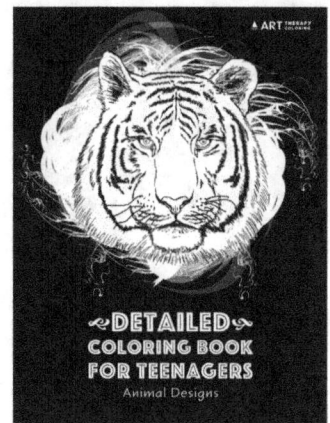

DETAILED
COLORING BOOK
FOR TEENAGERS
Animal Designs

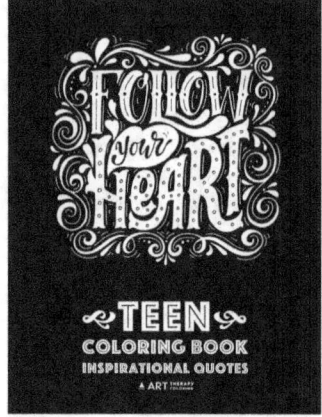

TEEN
COLORING BOOK
INSPIRATIONAL QUOTES

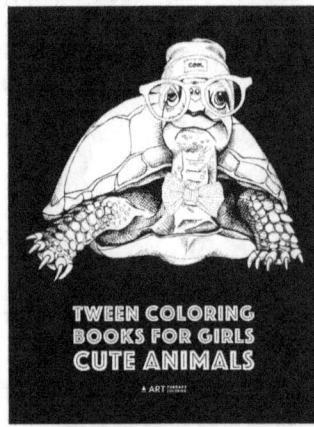

TWEEN COLORING
BOOKS FOR GIRLS
CUTE ANIMALS

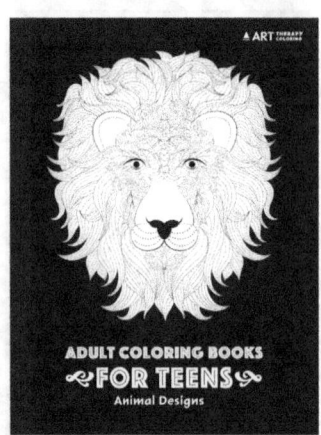

ADULT COLORING BOOKS
FOR TEENS
Animal Designs

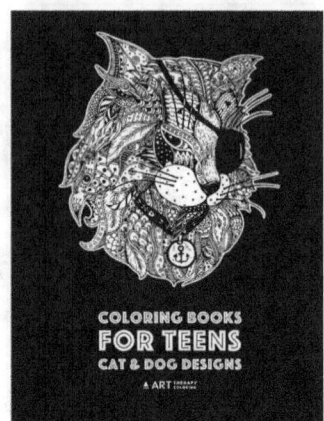

COLORING BOOKS
FOR TEENS
CAT & DOG DESIGNS

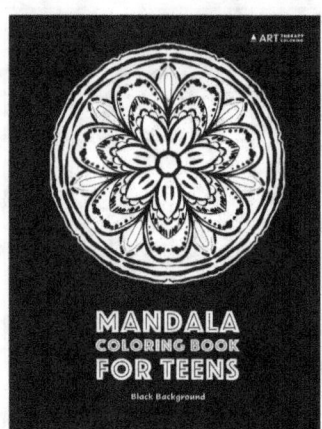

MANDALA
COLORING BOOK
FOR TEENS
Black Background

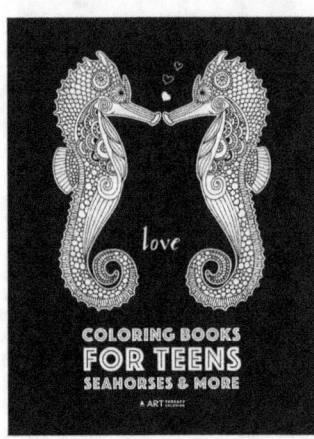

COLORING BOOKS
FOR TEENS
SEAHORSES & MORE

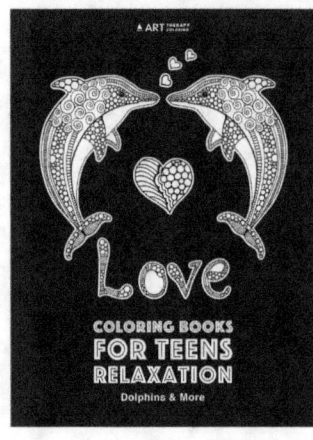

COLORING BOOKS
FOR TEENS
RELAXATION
Dolphins & More

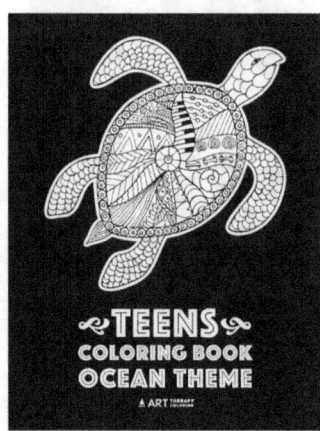

TEENS
COLORING BOOK
OCEAN THEME

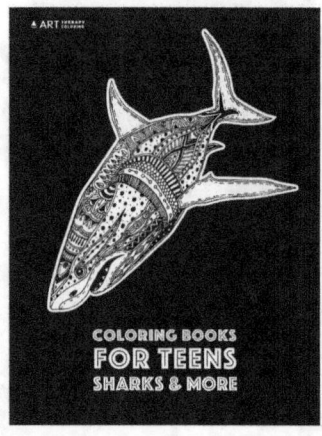

COLORING BOOKS
FOR TEENS
SHARKS & MORE

Art Therapy Coloring Books

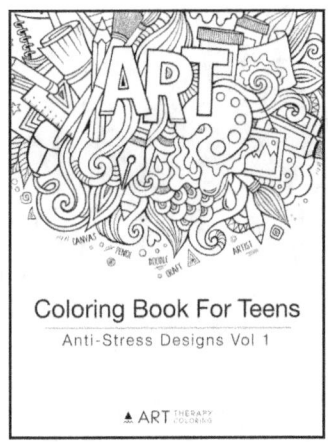

Coloring Book For Teens
Anti-Stress Designs Vol 1

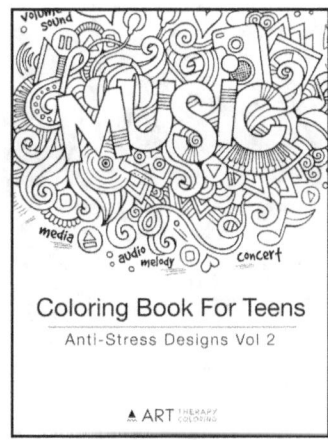

Coloring Book For Teens
Anti-Stress Designs Vol 2

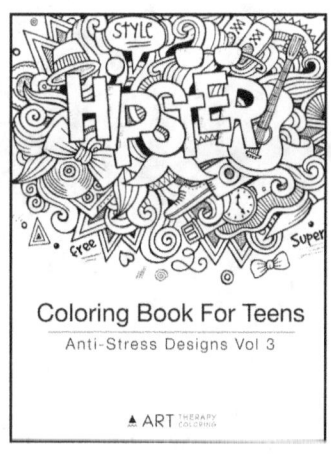

Coloring Book For Teens
Anti-Stress Designs Vol 3

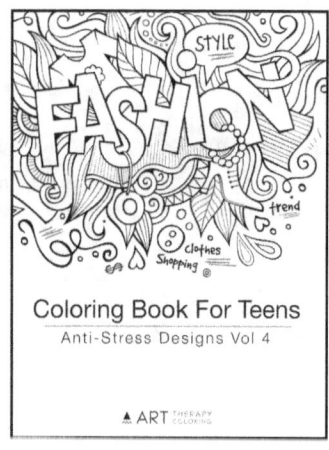

Coloring Book For Teens
Anti-Stress Designs Vol 4

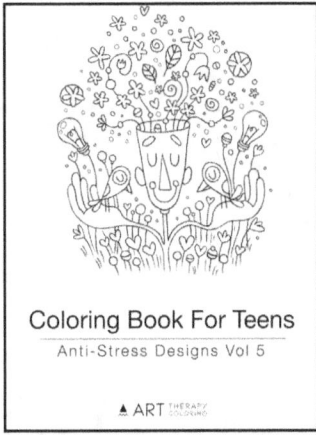

Coloring Book For Teens
Anti-Stress Designs Vol 5

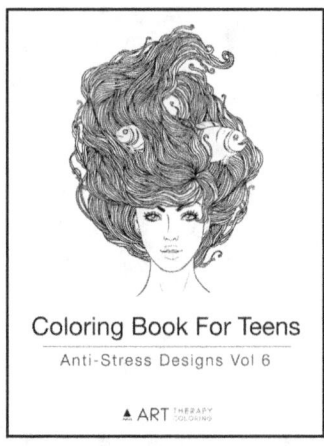

Coloring Book For Teens
Anti-Stress Designs Vol 6

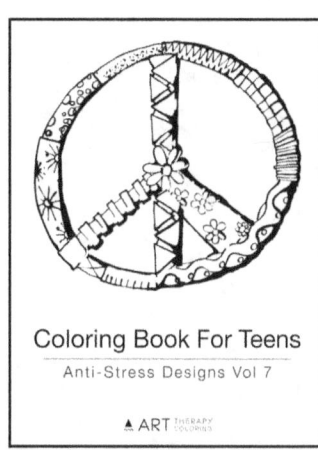

Coloring Book For Teens
Anti-Stress Designs Vol 7

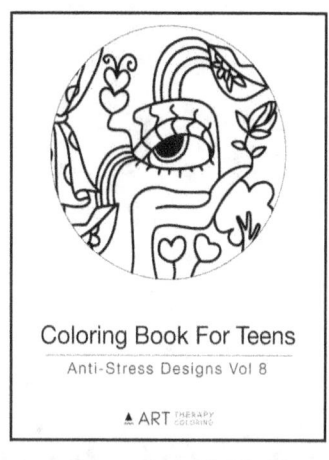

Coloring Book For Teens
Anti-Stress Designs Vol 8

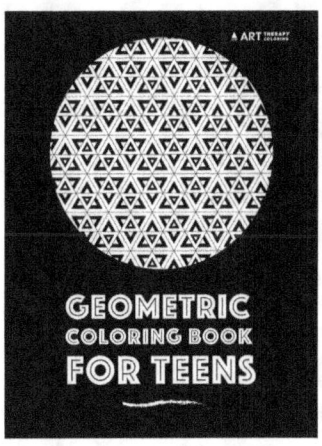

GEOMETRIC COLORING BOOK FOR TEENS

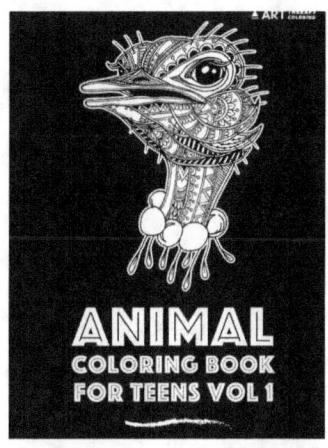

ANIMAL COLORING BOOK FOR TEENS VOL 1

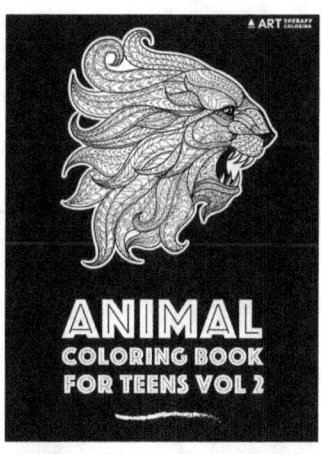

ANIMAL COLORING BOOK FOR TEENS VOL 2

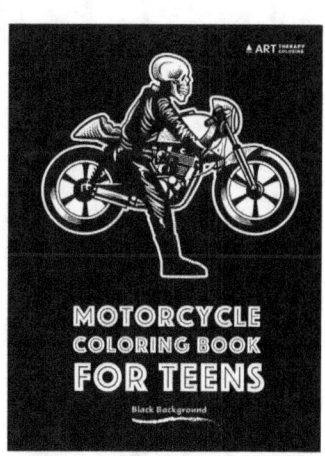

MOTORCYCLE COLORING BOOK FOR TEENS
Black Background

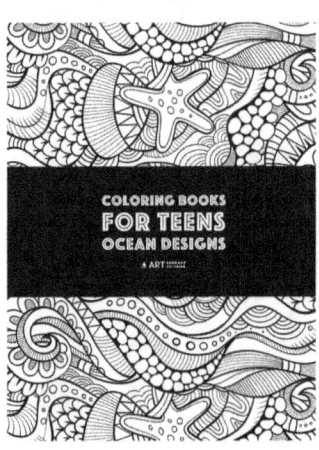

COLORING BOOKS FOR TEENS OCEAN DESIGNS

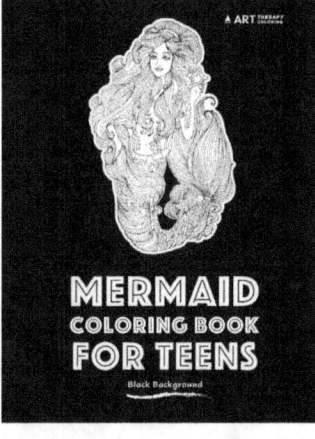

MERMAID COLORING BOOK FOR TEENS
Black Background

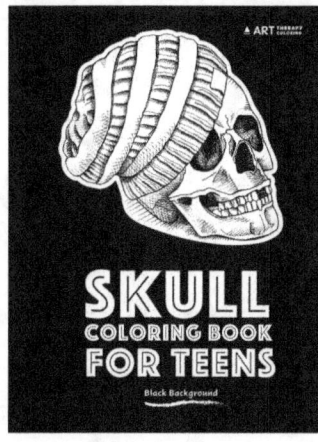

SKULL COLORING BOOK FOR TEENS
Black Background

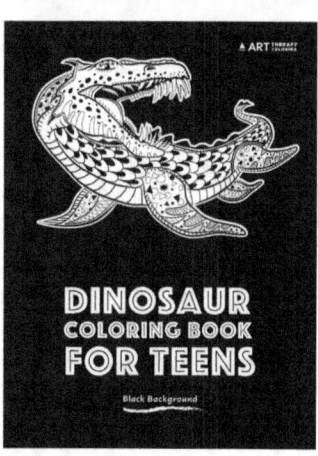

DINOSAUR COLORING BOOK FOR TEENS
Black Background

Dog & Coffee Coloring Book
For Adults

Published by:
Art Therapy Coloring
www.arttherapycoloring.com

ISBN: 978-1-944427-53-5

www.ingramcontent.com/pod-product-compliance
Lightning Source LLC
Chambersburg PA
CBHW082008230526
45468CB00023B/2831